T000150S

# THE
# GROVE

## A Nature Odyssey
## in 19½ Front Gardens

BEN DARK

ILLUSTRATIONS BY
SKEVOULLA GORDON

MITCHELL BEAZLEY

First published in Great Britain in 2022 by
Mitchell Beazley, an imprint of
Octopus Publishing Group Ltd
Carmelite House
50 Victoria Embankment
London EC4Y 0DZ
www.octopusbooks.co.uk

An Hachette UK Company
www.hachette.co.uk

First published in paperback in 2023

Copyright © Ben Dark 2022

Distributed in the US by Hachette
Book Group
1290 Avenue of the Americas
4th and 5th Floors
New York, NY 10104

Distributed in Canada by Canadian
Manda Group
664 Annette St.
Toronto, Ontario, Canada M6S 2C8

ISBN 978 1 78472 7413

A CIP catalogue record for this book is
available from the British Library.

Printed and bound in the UK

10 9 8 7 6 5 4 3 2 1

*To Katherine and Solomon*

# CONTENTS

Introduction *ix*

# INTRODUCTION

One autumn afternoon, the hedge outside No.67 Norroy Road changed my life. I say without glibness that nothing has affected me more. My baby son, for example, is perfect, but his arrival was not surprising. Those *Euonymus* came from nowhere.

They were the cultivar known as 'Emerald 'n' Gold'. If you have stood on a suburban street, you have seen it: banana-yellow leaves splashed with holly-green, an effect dismissed as 'colourful'. But that didn't matter. I recognized the shrubs and I could name them. The pavement had new meaning. It was no longer 'the bit outside 67', it was the pavement by the variegated *Euonymus fortunei*.

My second day at horticultural college had finished an hour earlier with twelve plant sprigs set in milk bottles and the instruction: 'memorize them'. Genus (*Euonymus*), followed by species (*fortunei*), followed by cultivar ('Emerald 'n' Gold'). And now one of those plants was in front of me, carrying with its garish leaves the obvious but somehow overlooked realization that every plant on Norroy Road had a name and was learnable.

I awoke to plants with a convert's zeal. Each week the dozen milk bottles and their twigs waited and I further deciphered the margins of Putney. I could speak a new language. My commute became circuitous. It took an extra forty minutes to reach our shared house, with detours to Fanthorpe Street, Erpingham Road and Clarendon Drive. My girlfriend waited while I scratched mahonia to show her wood the colour of turmeric, or crushed choisya to release the scent of vodka and basil. These were not rare plants, they grew on any street with gardens. Some I had certainly passed every day of my life, and yet I had let them remain undifferentiated. It was as if I had unquestioningly inhabited a city where people had no face, just a smooth balloon of flesh; and then one day I'd changed my spectacles and seen smiles everywhere.

I had not been unaware of nature. I knew an ash tree and a horse chestnut and I had a recipe for sloe gin. But I was plant-blind. Anything that was not emblematic or edible melted into a leafy backdrop. Sometimes bits of hedgerow would produce greengage plums, but I never learned about them from their foliage or their naked stems. It was easier to wait for the fruit and be surprised each time.

I grew up in Hampshire, at the foot of Shoulder of Mutton Hill, where a stone dedicated to Edward Thomas looks out on: 'Sixty miles of South Downs at one glance.' As a teenager I walked his woods, but in his poems I read the plants as rhythm and colour alone; a nice-sounding signifier for something fleeting or ancient. Hawthorn berry and hazel tuft, elm, celandine and charlock, words with as much meaning as his vanished manors of Codham, Cockridden and Childerditch.

Today I am a head gardener living in a flat in Southeast London with my wife and baby son. On the way here I have worked for museums, oligarchs and public parks. I have built rockeries from stones that arrive on their own lorries and pulled bindweed from the birthplace of the English Landscape Garden, but the joys of the city street and the memory of that first September on Norroy Road have not left me. Since discovering that gardeners tread a richer path than other folk, I have searched for more meaning in the plants I pass. I returned to the poems of my adolescence and reread them with unclouded eyes. I went back to university to study the history of gardens and took a further pay cut to spend my Thursdays looking through documents at the British Library and the Natural History Museum. I still feel fondly towards *Euonymus fortunei* 'Emerald 'n' Gold' but now the plant has layers of meaning beyond that first shock of recognition.

An outer layer tells of Robert Fortune, the botanist who defied the Qing Emperor and brought tea to the Himalayas. The species is named *fortunei* for him, but he introduced it as *Euonymus radicans*, receiving four pounds and four shillings for his variegated specimen in October 1863 at a sale in Stevens' Auction Rooms, an auction house dedicated to the sale of 'articles of zoological or scientific interest'.

Fortune's tea heist altered the economic future of China, Britain and India. The variegated *Euonymus* has altered only domestic hedges, so it is fitting that its discovery was entirely suburban. Fortune found it on a walk around Tokyo, having set off with 'a flask of wine slung over my shoulder, and a small loaf and jar of potted meat in my pocket'. Its discovery is a legacy of when the British Legation to Japan was home to more plant hunters than diplomats. But in it is also contained the story of England, a nation that regarded itself as the apogee of horticulture, being confronted by a gardening culture older and more complex than its own. As Fortune wrote, 'It is only a very few years since our taste in Europe led us to take an interest in and to admire those curious freaks of nature called variegated plants...the Japanese have been cultivating this taste for a thousand years.'

The cultivar 'Emerald 'n' Gold' was introduced in 1967 by the Corliss Brothers of Ipswich, Massachusetts. Like fellow '67 babies, the Twix bar and Angel Delight, it remains defiant in the face of fashion. Certainly, if all the plants of the English garden were lined up from the most cheerful to the most tasteful, with striped bedding petunias at one extreme and Vita Sackville-West's pure white 'Adélaïde d'Orléans' rose at the other, 'Emerald 'n' Gold' would be down with the rainbow fish mint. But I cherish it because it speaks of hope. It is an olive-bearing dove in the great flood of winter. Sometimes in early February I spot a lurid specimen in freshly dug soil and feel a rush of love for a householder I have never met, someone who endured colourless months of wet and cold and finally broke down, thinking, 'I don't bloody well care what I buy, just make it bright!'

It is these human stories that keep me enraptured by front gardens and make me choose Dudrich Mews over the Hampshire Hangers or other rural location. Nature writers are often cautioned not to anthropomorphize nature. 'Can gorse really feel malice?' ask their readers. 'Does the pine actually revel in its height over the heather?' But writing about domestic gardens begs for speculation on human emotion. Within those small squares are stories of ambition, envy, hope and failure. There is no box hedge beautiful enough to feel love, but there are plenty of people who love box hedging, love it enough to indulge in all the quixotic, self-wounding, doomed-lover pursuits that come with growing *Buxus* in the Southeast of England.

For all these reasons and more I have long believed that it would be possible to tell the story of my profession, my city and my passions from the pavement of one residential street. That is my intention in this book. Over the length of a suburban road and the course of a single year, I will set out everything I have learned in fifteen years of obsessing over gardens. History will unfold, not chronologically but in relation to this specific windowbox or that particular bay tree. The people I have met, in person or on pages, will live again in stems and twigs; the ghosts of plants I have loved, killed and longed for will loom over every fence and wall. All I need is a buddleja, so I can recount my lowest moments; a *Magnolia grandiflora*, to enable a few grandiloquent paragraphs; and a proper tree, for scale.

The road I have chosen is ten minutes' walk from my house.

It is Grove Park, and it needs no more introduction. Soon we will find out everything that is worth knowing about its plants and its people.

# I

## WISTERIA

*The subjugated seasons own thy power,*
*Waft all their sweets to decorate thy bower.*
Maurice Thomas, *Grove Hill*

At the summer end of London's driest-ever spring, my new son and I went up the hill to Camberwell. It was lunchtime in May, and Solomon slept in his pram, grumbling at the dreams that visit babies. I distractedly looked about, preoccupied with figures and train times, trying to find a blend of work and childcare that kept us housed, solvent and guilt-free. It was a pointless endeavour: Kat and I had already played through every late start and early finish and had decided on three days per week at a nursery near the station.

This walk was a pre-enactment. We were timing the school run. It was seventeen minutes from our flat to the nursery gate, but that was up the big hill by Sainsbury's, past petrol stations, off-licences and four lanes of traffic. I was testing Route B, which crossed Goose Green, its grass still fresh in the shade of the plane trees, skirted a churchyard hung with climbing roses and ran along Grove Park.

Everything was shortened by the noonday sun. The pram's awning cast no shade on the little legs protruding from it and my journey had been an inefficient zig-zag, which crossed and recrossed back roads, trundling out from the shadow of a wall to the cover of a hawthorn avenue and back over to the lee of a privet hedge.

For many plants, life in the heat appeared futile. The flower beds were clearly too small, the quantity of tarmac and brick too vast. How could the little pink-leaved hebes of Peckham and Camberwell survive all the sky between dawn and dusk? There are some gardens that make the parched observer uncomfortable to look at. But others bring their own cool, even at midday. They exist next to the spaces of bare soil and prickly heat, but seem to do so at a lower temperature. The effect is dependent on shadow, and shadows come from having variations in height. In the scorching summers that are becoming the norm in Britain, the plants of a flat garden resemble little soldiers on parade, sent out to fry in full dress. Gardens with a mixed canopy create their own understorey. In the bruised-blue shade, flowers and herbs are recast as fronds on a forest floor. There is a mystery and allure in gloom, an invitation for the viewer to create a story: it's why the ambiguous cowboy hides his eyes in a Stetson's shade.

So ran my thoughts as I happily put aside the household budget and stopped outside No.91 Grove Park. This wisteria-draped house is one half of a pair of semi-detached villas from the late nineteenth century. In an 1873 notice of auction, houses on this road are described as 'built in a very substantial manner', language designed to appeal to the Victorian patriarch. Substance was crucial to such a man. This was the peak of London's suburban expansion. The middle classes were leaving the centre of town to live in new, brick-built family homes on the fringes. But with the mortar drying on so many fresh neighbourhoods, and the new ability for clerks, artisans and other undesirables to reach their employment by train or tram, there was always a danger that the villa next door would not sell, would be broken down into several residences or, even worse, into 'rooms' as the quickest way for an absent landlord to realize their profit. Whoever bought No.91 would have known that Camberwell was a neighbourhood on the slide. Its bubble of genteel remoteness had been punctured by the rails of the locomotive. The grand four-storey Georgian terraces were already splitting, like cells, into ever-more apartments.

The building before me was a reaction to this, still shouting about its own substantiality 150 years later.

The house was inviting in a way that its mirrored neighbour was not. The front doors were feet from each other, their porches divided by a simple wall and corniced pillar, but No.92 was a mass of hot brick and No.91 a place of cool and inviting refuge. The difference lay in the shade of a mature wisteria. It crept out from the corner of the house, linking it to the heavily wooded railway sidings beyond and anchoring it to nature in a way no hedge could. The bay windows below were dark, and spoke of a hinterland not possible behind panes of glass in full sun.

The plant was *Wisteria sinensis*, the Chinese wisteria. It is one of two species commonly grown in Europe. The other is *Wisteria floribunda*, the Japanese wisteria. Those who wish to tell them apart (once the flowers have faded) must remember that *floribunda* twines up a drainpipe from right to left, whereas *sinensis* does so from left to right. A trick I used in my early days in horticulture was to hold my hands with thumbs and forefingers curved into a 'C' for Chinese, and a round-bottomed 'J' for Japanese. An imagined marble rolling down from finger to thumb gives the direction of travel and the origin of the plant, and the whole process makes it appear as if one is taking a picture with an invisible camera.

The Chinese wisteria is my favourite of the two. Its flower clusters are not as long as those of *W. floribunda* but they open all at once, huge and fat, like watercolour grapes on a wine bottle's label. The Japanese wisteria may have two-and-a-half feet of hanging bloom, but it opens sequentially from the raceme's top to bottom. For a shaded wisteria walk, with dripping icicles of petal that brush the heads of visitors, then choose *floribunda*, but be aware that the flowers will be out at the same time as the leaves. *Sinensis*, on the other hand, flowers on naked and gnarled stems. In late April, when the content creators of social media come to London, it is the Chinese wisteria they hunt through Chelsea and Notting Hill. Nothing brings engagement like a veil of amethyst on a white stucco wall.

Budding from seemingly veteran wood gives *Wisteria sinensis* a uniquely gothic appeal. It has the poet's ability to play the tortured ancient from youth. The stems bite into each other as they twist. Constricted growth bulges and flattens. Its wood quickly becomes striated, as if the thin bark lies over a mass of knotted tendon and muscle. It is why the wisteria is such a potent symbol of haunting. It is something decrepit and half-ruined but capable of transforming into a being of otherworldly beauty, like the Yuxa of Tatar mythology, the hundred-year-old serpent who lounges as a lean young boy or girl to seduce the unwary. It is why Charlotte Perkins Gilman called her best ghost story *The Giant Wistaria* and why only that plant's roots could embrace the horrific secret at the tale's heart.

Wisteria germinate only to climb. They are the King Kongs of the plant world, capable of scaling trees and pulling them to the ground, of swallowing the sides of mountains. To the plant that decorates No.91, the house is nothing; a boulder to be vaulted in search of something greater. Without constant clipping it would be at the eaves in a single season.

I once took over the gardening of a half-timbered house in the English commuter belt. The one thing that elevated it from the stockbrokers' mansions in the surrounding cul-de-sacs was the magnificent wisteria on its frontage. The owner had nurtured the plant for years, pruning assiduously to the Royal Horticultural Society's recommended regime: a reduction of new growth to five buds in July, then down to two in February. After working with the family for a few years, I found some reason to enter the loft above the stairs and to my horror found it stuffed full of the dried and grasping tendrils of summers past, clipped off from the outside and left to wither into nightmare spaghetti. For decades the plant had been worming its way into the architecture, waiting for the happy season when the gardener turned his back and it could lift the tiles from the roof, haul down the timbers and romp free.

As a boy I instinctively took the side of the wisteria in its battle with the built environment. I have memories of willing my parents' plant to reach the telephone wires and race along them. I suspect that my sympathies still lie in that direction – certainly my favourite wisteria in London is nothing like the much-photographed examples on the white walls of Cheyne Walk. Mine grows on the corner of Eccleston Square in the shadow of Victoria Station. Some years ago it slipped the secateurs of its attendants and escaped, vaulting through the branches of a mahonia and up into the limbs of a towering London plane tree. Up there its flowers hang like flags in a ruined ship's rigging. It has thrown down ropes for itself to climb and is belaying towards distant canopies. Even with nowhere left to scale it throws itself optimistically upwards, as if it would snare the clouds over Pimlico and drag itself into a realm beyond.

The trick to growing wisteria up into a tree is to ignore your impulse to plant it next to the trunk. Instead, plant the wisteria in a hole at the drip-line, that is, at the point where the shelter of the canopy ends and the soil changes from dry to wet after the spring storms. Here the light is strongest and the twigs at their drooping, fully extended lowest. Be aware that the vine will be drawn to the southerly side of a tree. Over years it will tangle there, until it is a great green dreadlock. A vast, unruly solar panel that will eventually topple its host. Were this to happen to the tree that holds my favourite wisteria, it would fall onto the roofs of Warwick Way, and from there it's only a few short twists around the chimney pots to Warwick Square and St Gabriel's, where it could meet the Virginia creeper that has already claimed that church.

This vision of a wisteria rising from the smashed boughs of the tree that held it is no mere fantasy. The plants have evolved for just this occurrence. There is an unusual flexibility to a wisteria's stem. When scientists at Duke University subjected woody material to stress, they found wisteria unique in experiencing creep under flexural loading, which is to say, it did not snap. It bent and stayed bent. At work I grow standard wisterias, a single stem grown up a thick stake to unfurl umbrella-like in an approximation of a real tree's canopy. One morning I arrived on the heels of a summer squall to find the stakes had snapped. Without support the wisteria had folded like men without spines, the tops of their heads resting forlornly on the ground next to their still-upright ankles. Other plants would have shattered but the wisteria was ready to grow onwards, happy to live with an arch in its trunk like the loop in a sea serpent's back.

In writing this book I made a happy discovery. I had wanted to find out if the houses of Grove Park were as obviously High Victorian as they appeared, and so turned to the archives. In a winter 2006 edition of *Garden History*, I found an article titled 'Dr John Coakley Lettsom; Plant Collector of Camberwell' and learned that my beloved Grove Park had not been built on the straggling fields that separated the swallowed villages of Dulwich, Peckham and Camberwell. Fantastically, it lay on the site of one of Georgian London's most celebrated and eccentric gardens: Grove Hill, inspiration for a thousand poems, pamphlets and fashionable day-trips. The lines that opened this chapter, *The subjugated seasons own thy power / Waft all their sweets to decorate thy bower*, were written in 1799 by the antiquarian Maurice Thomas as part of a descriptive ode to Grove Hill, a long-form poem that led the reader in rhyming couplets between the temples, fountains and miniature observatories of Dr Lettsom's green Elysium.

Lettsom was a remarkable man. The abolitionist son of a plantation owner, he was born on the island of Tortola, where he freed his slaves the moment he inherited them, before travelling to the Netherlands. His thesis on the natural history of tea earned him a doctorate in medicine from Leiden University and he set up in London as an energetic and philanthropic dispensing surgeon. Among his many achievements, he founded the Medical Society of London and drove the quack Dr Meyersbach, who had grown rich sniffing out fictional ailments in the urine of bishops and actors, from the capital.

The red brick villa at Grove Hill was demolished in 1890 and Nos.9 to 12 Grove Park now stand on its site (we will get to them later when it is time to talk of camellias and laburnum; we must remember that we are still at the other end of the street where the sun beats down and Solomon sleeps on). No.91, with wisteria darkening its door, is built on the ground that was once Lettsom's Temple of Sibyl. This was ever a viney place. Lettsom wrote that the temple 'is supported by the trunks of eighteen oak trees; round each ivy, virgin's bower honey-suckles or other climbing shrubs entwine their foliage, and meet at their summits in the style of festoons.'

How the Doctor would have loved wisteria. Historians discourage counterfactual histories but as a daydreamer on a city pavement, most of my thoughts start 'what if' or 'suppose that'. Suppose that Lettsom had not been forced to sell Grove Hill in 1810. What if he had not died in 1815 but had lived just one more year? Would we have seen the first Chinese wisteria in Europe growing here? I think it possible. Two plants arrived in London in 1816 on separate East India Company ships. One found its way to Peckham, at the other end of the road from us, resting briefly with John Reeves before moving to its home seven miles away in the Bromley house of Thomas Carey Palmer. Remarkably, the other wisteria also ended up exactly seven miles from Grove Hill at Wood Lodge, the estate of gardener and merchant Charles Hampden Turner. These were gifts given by young adventurers to comfortable, elder gentlemen of scientific leanings. Lettsom was the botanical patron par excellence. He wrote a book on the subject: *The Naturalist's and Traveller's Companion,* a primer on botany for company men heading overseas. He noted that before its publication he 'had kept it by him for some time in manuscript, and occasionally given copies to sea-faring persons, and such of his acquaintance going abroad'.

Lettsom advised those in search of 'vegetable productions' to cast their nets wide: 'the sea and its shore, deep running waters, dikes, marshes, moors, mountains, cultivated and barren fields, woods, rocks etc afford each their peculiar plants'. The first wisteria on English soil were taken from nowhere so wild. Both originated in the garden of a Cantonese merchant named

Pan Changyao, rooted cuttings struck from a plant brought to the city by Changyao's nephew Tinqua. The young man may have found it growing rampant in the forests of Fujian or Jiangxi, but more likely he procured it from a tea garden in the city of Zhangzhou; here the record blurs and the origins are lost. What we do know is that almost every English wisteria is descended by whip, scion, layer or seed from those two plants that arrived in 1816. It may have taken two hundred years, but *Wisteria sinensis* has finally reached Lettsom's bower.

I looked at my watch and pushed the pram on. We had been out for nearly half an hour and I needed to get going, but I still paused outside No.92, the house next door. Growing on the corner was a tiny noodle-thin *Wisteria sinensis*. The soil around it was wet and freshly watered and a hopeful wire snaked up and then across the red brick. If imitation is the sincerest form of flattery, then someone was paying an earnest compliment to their neighbour. Some day, sooner than we might think, the wisterias of 92 and 91 Grove Park will meet and tangle above the corniced pillar that divides the houses, uniting them under a great, green moustache of leaf and flower.

# 2

# PRIVET

I once stepped from our front door to find a spring burbling from the pavement. It was as clear as glass and very beautiful, a pool with little bits of rose and basalt grit rolling in and out of an invisible water column. I reported it on the service company's website (select one of the following options: 'a small puddle is beginning to form; a large puddle is forming; there is a large body of water that is interfering with traffic; a huge amount of water is putting people at risk') and someone came to paint an arrow on the curb. Over subsequent days the arrow was joined by dashes and numbers. A tangle of lines spread out from the pool and moved off down the road. They stopped two houses away where a section of tarmac was circled and then crossed. And next, less than a week from the spring's arrival, I came home to find the ground gone and the raw water pipe exposed. I never saw a worker or highway engineer. It was urban magic – as if the symbols had writhed and multiplied and finally blasted down through the subsoil under their own power.

Up on the hill, Grove Park is usually covered in similar mysterious circles and stripes. Roadwork hieroglyphs. Red is for electricity, blue for water and yellow for gas. There is no particular colour for sewage pipes, they are just noted in the white used for 'any other business'. To be an expert reader of these symbols must be an extraordinary thing. To such a person, the tarmac would be transparent and the arterial pipes visible, each of them bristling with service ducts like a street-long centipede.

The dot of paint outside No.71 is different from the other markings. It is an overdubbed splodge, reapplied over decades in the exact same spot in blue, green and red paint. It is a message from one man to himself: *stand here*. That man is the celebrated artist and Royal Academician Tom Phillips. For fifty years he has returned annually to Grove Park in the last week of May, resprayed the mark on the pavement and taken a photograph of the house opposite – No.102. In each picture, a London plane tree leans in from stage left. In 1973 it is slim, taller than the house behind but still fresh and light. Over the years the trunk thickens and flares. Strange knobbles appear and develop into paunchy outgrowths. The tree coats itself in excess wood that serves no obvious purpose. It spreads into middle age. Anyone encountering the plane would assume it had been sucking up the car fumes and city sun for two hundred years; without Tom's photographs they could not know how young and smooth it had been in their own lifetimes.

Apart from the tree, the images are remarkable in their mundanity. In the first photograph, the house stands solid and semi-detached, its bay window dark against the spring sunshine. Half a century on, nothing has changed. The same six panes of glass sit in the same front door. The fretwork of the porch remains pristine and white, as does the woodwork of the lintels on the first floor. Even the lamppost is the same, though it was painted black in 1995 and now holds a sign explaining that parking is only for permit holders 'Q' between Monday and Friday, 11am to 1pm. A privet hedge (*Ligustrum ovalifolium*) separates the house from the road and another runs along the path, a neat barrier between the garden and its neighbour.

The photographs set my heart racing. Ageing trees have the same flavour as melting candles – a visual umami, savoury and satisfying. But while wax goes from pillar to pool in the course of a dinner party, a tree might take two hundred years to transform. We must chase their changes through paintings, postcards and yellowing prints. Prior to finding Tom's project, titled *20 Sites n Years* (nineteen other unremarkable local views have also been documented), the best way to see plane trees maturing had been to search the archives for 'view from Waterloo Bridge' and look for the plantings on Joseph Bazalgette's Victoria Embankment. There is a thrill in watching the head-high saplings (set far too close) thicken as the horse-drawn carriages are replaced by double-decker trams and the penny boats steam endlessly by.

But the Embankment is just too far from Waterloo Bridge and the planes too numerous. Go and look now, they are still there; the impression will be of a line of trees to complement the line of road to the left and the line of water to the right. To really appreciate a tree's ageing, it needs to be seen up close. Here on Grove Park was the chance to witness some truly idiosyncratic ageing. I began to search for the genesis of a particular knobble in the tree's bark, flicking back and forth between 1973 and 1982 when the tree was first pollarded, then forward ten years to 1992 when it was pruned again, then on to the pollard-heavy years of 2008, 2013, 2016, then back to the early 1970s. Then I saw it – all through the growth and cutbacks, the swelling and the leaf drops, the hedge behind sat unchanging. Age had not touched the privet.

In that moment my perspective on gardens changed. After years of tramping the city streets, I thought I was immune to the wild shifts in relativity I suffered on the day I stepped out of horticultural college, but I was once again experiencing immersion into a deeper world. The next morning I went to Grove Park and pretended to tie my shoelaces outside No.102. Behind the low fence the stems of these half-century-old plants were unremarkable. They started in a thick bole from which straight stems extended; not quite green, not quite brown, the colour of algae on an untreated fence. Among the living were numerous dried and dead branches. Here was the secret of the privet's unnatural youth. It was constantly replacing itself, sending up stems and letting them meet the hedge-cutter for a few summers before giving up and starting again with new wood. For years I had been walking the suburban streets trying to guess the age of spreading magnolias and twisted wisterias, without knowing that the oldest and likely original plantings were those that I had most commonly overlooked, the plain privet hedges.

I am not the first to dismiss privet. The plant is a symbol for all that is small-minded and suburban, the growing embodiment of that awful phrase, 'We keep ourselves to ourselves round here.' The world's all-time bestselling book series opens with a tautology: 'Mr and Mrs Dursley, of number four, Privet Drive, were proud to say that they were perfectly normal, thank you very much.' J K Rowling could have ended the sentence at Privet Drive, and let the readers infer the self-proclaimed normality. As early as 1900, the author Roma White was able to speak with confidence of a species of small-minded suburbanite: 'Their horticultural horizon is bounded by privet, and their out-look be-ribboned with lobelias.'

Vita Sackville-West, a woman of true genius and our greatest-ever writer of Sunday gardening columns (or 'those beastly little *Observer* articles', as she would have them), hated privet. A reader once asked how to enliven a dull privet hedge and was recommended: '*Clematis montana*, either the ordinary white kind or its pale pink variety...Then I would have wisteria, either the ordinary mauve or the more exquisite white... Then I would have some of the autumn-colouring vines, the magnificent huge-leaved *Vitis coignetiae*, for instance, bright pink in September.'

This is absurd. Vita transparently wanted that hedge dead.

*Clematis montana* swallows trees and tumbles down Afghan mountains, while *Vitis coignetiae,* with its leaves as big as a kitchen clock, is food for hungry bears. Both are beautiful beyond measure, and the vine in particular should be more familiar in our cities and gardens, but to suggest them for a privet hedge is akin to recommending a double avenue of lime trees for the reader's garden path. We should not be surprised, this was a woman who, when giving advice on designing small gardens, cheerfully added: 'By a small garden I mean anything from half an acre to two acres.'

The creator of Sissinghurst Castle Garden was a snob. As a bisexual in a repressed age she railed against the hypocrisy of her peers and looked forward to a world where she and others like her (she knew there were many) could be candid and at least recognized, if not celebrated. Such enlightened sentiment did not colour her view of the working and middle classes. I am a Sackville-West devotee but it is as clear as Kentish sky that when she calls privet 'such nasty hedges' and writes: 'I am all for playing rough with things that play rough with us, for making them behave as our servants, not our masters,' she is talking about both the plant and the kind of people who lived behind it. After all, this was a woman who penned a letter to her husband, the diplomat Harold Nicolson, complaining:

I hate democracy. I hate la populace. I wish education had never been introduced. I don't like tyranny, but I like an intelligent oligarchy. I wish la populace had never been encouraged to emerge from its rightful place. I should like to see them as well fed and well housed as T. T. cows, but no more articulate than that.

What would Sackville-West have thought of my adopted gardens? Grove Park was built for the Victorian cattle class but beauty, eccentricity, personality and brilliance all have a place here, if not in the houses then certainly in the hedges. At the top of the road there is a handsome three-storey house with servants' stairs and white stucco walls. It sits behind a thick and unbroken line of snowberry (*Symphoricarpos albus*), a plant more common to the winnowed shrubberies of London's fading parks. On the Grove it is sweet-natured and surprising. Summer sees it soft green, with leaves that bruise black like spinach. By December it is bare and twiggy, its branches pearled with pure white berries, the whole thing a stylized blizzard through a miniature forest. Down the road grows another eccentric American: *Mahonia × media*, the Oregon grape, a plant as spiny and dark as a movie dinosaur, with bright yellow wood beneath its bark, and berries blue-black with juice like cartridge ink. At No.37 there is an entire plot bordered with *Muehlenbeckia complexa*, a strange, black-stemmed, tiny-leaved, sprawling, scrambling thing from New Zealand, utterly useless as a hedge but indicative of some serious horticultural ambition. The hedges of Grove Park are complex, wonderful and occasionally dreadful. I'm sure their owners are too.

I work in the Chiltern Hills. The garden is on a semi-private road with houses for people who were once big in companies you've heard of. Vita would have hated them. In 1934 her husband visited the chairman of J P Morgan in his house on the Hudson River. He wrote to her of the garden: 'It was all typically American millionaire...just mown grass and neat trees. All very good taste and depressing. No inner reality.' The description tallies perfectly with what I pass on my morning cycle from Beaconsfield station. Is there reality behind those electric gates? Hard to say. They are all retired now, the residents of these recessed mansions, but they seem happy when glimpsed at the wheel of a huge car or out walking an old labrador.

Their hedges are perfect. Mostly they are beech – big, square-topped blocks, trimmed four times a year by respectable garden maintenance companies with tripod ladders and sign-written vans. The trees above are also beech. Before this was an executive enclave, it was the grounds of a larger house. Before that it was a chalk-topped escarpment, the type that sheltered charcoal men and wood turners. A few veteran trees survive and their wild branches drip down to touch the crisp corners of the hedges below. In high summer it seems impossible that the geometric hedges are related to the grey-trunked giants above. They are the same species but the difference in shape and scale makes a connection between them absurd.

In winter the contrast is yet more stark. The trees are bare, the hedges mussed with a coat of dry leaves. Beech is partially marcescent; it holds spent leaves until spring. Sexually mature branches denude, juvenile branches remain dressed. Trimming the hedges takes away the plant's twig tips and so its chance to flower and bear fruit, thus the hedge-cutters keep these plants in permanent adolescence. It is a sort of vegetable castration and, like mammalian castration, the effects are chemical as well as physical. Hormones crucial to the leaf drop are not produced and the plants remain like the privet on Grove Park – fifty or sixty years old and still dressed in their childhood garb.

In *On the Making of Gardens*, Sir George Sitwell states that 'architecture, the most unselfish of arts, belongs to the passerby.' I agree. Making the walker look at an oversized SUV where a magnolia, holly or flowering cherry could stand is a deeply ungenerous act. Luckily, on Grove Park there are no electric gates and little off-street parking. Instead, both sides of the road are lined with cars. It is not an ideal situation but it means there is always some garden to look at. And the ugly vehicles tell their own stories. Generally they are tales of middle-class family life: child seats, bike racks and National Trust stickers in the windows, badges that would have identified their drivers to Vita Sackville-West as 'frequenters of main roads', town people in the habit of popping off to look at (and misunderstand) the most obvious bits of the English countryside.

I suspect Vita's hatred of privet was exaggerated for effect. Her hatred of the National Trust appears to have been heartfelt and genuine. The archaic code of feudal primogeniture by which her family lived saw Knole, Vita's ancestral home and perhaps her one true love (surpassing Sissinghurst and Harold, Virginia Woolf and Violet Trefusis), pass to an uncle on her father's death. That uncle, Major-General Charles John Sackville-West, began negotiations to grant Knole to the National Trust in 1935. In 1946 the freehold to the house and walled garden was handed over. It was too much for Vita, who never came to terms with the public's intrusion into what she regarded as her birthright. In 1958, thirty years after she had been forced out and twenty years after the decision was made to preserve the house for the nation, she wrote to her husband:

> I drove back from Sevenoaks through the park at Knole…I had better not go on writing about it because it is making me cry…Oh Hadji Hadji – why do I love Knole so much? It's stupid – and I hate that beastly Nat. Trust symbol. Knole should have been mine, mine, mine. We were meant for each other.

When her son raised the possibility of Sissinghurst going to the Trust she was coldly furious, writing in her diary:

> Never, never, never. Not that hard little plate at my door. Nigel can do what he likes when I am dead, but as long as I live no Nat. Trust or any other foreign body shall have my darling. Over my corpse or my ashes; not otherwise. It is bad enough to have lost my Knole but they shan't take [Sissinghurst] from me. That at least is my own.

Sissinghurst, of course, is now a National Trust property, visited by people from Beaconsfield and Grove Park, Japan and Charleston. The hard little plates are everywhere. But on the wall of the South Cottage, an ancient climbing rose, 'Madame Alfred Carrière', still grows. It was the first thing Vita and Harold planted, reportedly before the deeds for the ruined place had been signed. As a plant touched by the great lady herself, it has become a place of informal pilgrimage. How many cuttings has it lost? How many gentlemen have left with their thighs bleeding and their pockets full of surreptitious thorns? How many handbags have smuggled it out across the home counties?

There is cash to be made selling clones of this plant. Other plants in the National Trust's care have also felt the hand of genius, enough for a whole money-spinning collection, available online and in gift shops. After Vita Sackville-West's climbing rose I would suggest adding Paul McCartney's privet to the range, taking us neatly from the White Garden to *The White Album* and incidentally telling the story of a century.

No.20 Forthlin Road, McCartney's childhood home, is an ex-council house in the Liverpool suburb of Allerton. It was bought by the Trust in 1995 and stuffed full of things indicative of 1950s working-class life. Someone went to the trouble of tracking down an original Hoover Junior model 119 in brown and gold to decorate the understairs cupboard. None of these objects were actually owned by the McCartneys but they would surely have recognized them. However, bricks and roof tiles aside, there is one original feature. The privet hedge. It is the same one planted when the house was built in 1949, the same one glimpsed in the Beatles' very first photo shoots, I know that now. Like the one at No.102 Grove Park, it is an unassuming immortal.

Vita Sackville-West died at home at Sissinghurst on the 2nd of June 1962, with her beloved rose in full flower. Four days later the Beatles played 'Love Me Do' at Abbey Road Studios, a song written by a grammar school boy behind a privet hedge on Forthlin Road. The Beatles signed to EMI and the kids went wild. In 1967, the same year the National Trust took Vita's Sissinghurst, Paul McCartney rode a white horse through a ruined arch at her beloved Knole. The moment is captured in the video for 'Penny Lane', a song about bus stops and barbers' shops beneath the blue suburban skies. La populace had emerged and there would be no putting them back.

# 3

## BUDDLEJA

Somewhere above the railway, Chadwick Road becomes Grove Park. Where exactly does not matter; whichever way you cut it, the first plant on the street is a butterfly bush (*Buddleja*). They line the tracks and whisker the bridge, creeping up through a scree of sycamore and bramble to poke at the adjoining gardens, half-obscuring a sign warning that this zone is under the control of 'The Land Sheriffs'. On the territory of these lawmen, shrubs grow through a mulch of fading cider cans and nod every nine minutes at a passing train. Welcome to buddleja country.

Buddleja is such a railway plant that it shocks when met in an herbaceous border. But what a good plant it is when standing plump and pruned above the phlox and phlomis.

In full bloom its giraffe tongues of pointed mauve and mass of silver-backed leaves rival any of the glamour plants that surround it. In September the blow-torched old flowers look ancient and Australian, like a brown banksia or a fruited callistemon, but if the seeds are off-putting, then the plant can simply be deadheaded. It is perverse we reserve deadheading for roses when buddleja is just as eager to impress with fresh buds and stems.

The garden writer Christopher Lloyd placed *Buddleja davidii* in the first tier of second-rate shrubs. On Grove Park it grows in the truly third-rate locations, in the mortar of the bridge, of course, but also quite beautifully in a stony wedge of almost-flower bed between the bins at No.24; in a small plastic pot at No.44, so ancient that moss and liverwort have welded it to the path; and tangled up with a yellow bamboo at No.77. In China, three in every hundred buddlejas are mutants with pure white flowers. We even have one of those, a second-year plant growing from a brick pillar at the centre of the bridge.

The road has one garden in which buddleja grows as an undoubted king. At No.104, its twisted trunk has forced aside the paving slabs in an otherwise empty courtyard. It is a giant, dense and floriferous, soaring above the wall and taking up space that could be used for a car or even a few motorbikes.

Hearteningly, it has numerous old scars and stubbed branches, the relics of historic pruning. They show that the plant has been interacted with. There was a thought process that ended, 'I must cut back that purple plant' and not, 'I must get rid of that thing so I can see more patio.' It's not yet indicative of a passion for horticulture, but fires ignite from smaller sparks. A single large buddleja could become a large buddleja and a flower pot, from where it is a small hop to five flower pots and a large buddleja, then ten flower pots and a skip full of concrete paving slabs. The plant's mere survival hints at a gardener as yet unawakened.

Buddleja owes its success in colonizing these almost-places to the shape of its seeds. Our greatest observer of invasive weeds, Sir Edward Salisbury, found that in a sheltered building, buddleja seeds took an average of five-and-a-half seconds to fall ten feet. This is nothing compared to rosebay willowherb's, which wafted down over 43 seconds, but those seeds are fluffy parachutes and buddleja's are wings. Take an albatross to a still room and drop it from a ladder and you will know that winged things need wind to ride. We must imagine what those five-and-a-half seconds might extend to when met with the induced airflow and turbulent wake of a speeding train or the mad vortexes of an urban canyon. For each buddleja rooted in the seam of a city chimney, ten thousand seeds missed the crack and swooped down in the building's lee, dropping on pavements, gardens and the heads of passing people. If we Londoners slept on mounds of shale, we would all plant buddleja within a year.

Sir Edward understood humans as vectors for spreading plants. During and after the Blitz, he studied the vegetation of London's new ruins. He found ferns growing in the nave of St James's Piccadilly, where Wren's shattered plasterwork lay under tumbled walls in vaults filled by the fireman's hose. Rosebay willowherb empurpled the city. Salisbury found it on 88 per cent of bomb sites, noting its preference for land that had been recently scorched. But he was aware that its spread outside London had begun twenty years earlier, something he attributed to the rise of the motorcar and with it the picnicker, who, in constant need of hot tea, was wont to light small fires and sip nervously as they blazed out of control.

This was a man with the perfect mind for daydreaming about plants. He was able to identify turned-up trousers as a vector for weed spread. The little fabric flaps swished through the undergrowth at the height of a flowering stem, collecting and storing seeds like a gardener's envelope, before dropping them on a subsequent walk. He did not directly blame Edward VII for the spread of black plantain from the footpath to the beet field, but since the king singlehandedly popularized the turn-up, we, Salisbury's readers, can make that accusation.

Muddy boots were a preoccupation. Sir Edward swept the dust from beneath church pews and strew it on sterile soil. From his sowings he grew iron grass, frog rush, pearlwort and daisies, and all this from a congregation in their Sunday brogues. Salisbury wondered about the feet of the Romans. The legionary's hobnailed sandal was the perfect ride for a mud-borne seed. There was, of course, the dirt between the soldiers' toes, but also the junctions in the leather thongs and the pinch point where metal studs met the sole. A twenty-mile march is forty thousand footsteps. That's forty thousand potential pick ups and set downs per man. Plants spread in mysterious ways.

The first shrub I ever pruned for a stranger was a self-seeded buddleja of a similar size to the one growing at No.104. I was at horticultural college and living with my girlfriend in a house full of Australians. We needed money for rent and targeted the smart streets nearby with horticultural flyers. The design was striking: a sixteenth-century woodcut of a man standing on a spade under the wishful headline 'Ben Dark: Gardener'. The back was a photograph of me, grinning and floppy-haired near a camellia bush, with my phone number alongside. They were a surprise hit and one of the first people who called wanted their whole garden redone ('Yes, yes, of course that's something I could manage') in weekly two-hour chunks ('Yes, I think two hours should be plenty'), starting with cutting back an overgrown buddleja ('Oh yes, I'm sure this is the perfect time for the job').

I hung up, suddenly insecure. Two hours was plenty of time to discover that I was moonlighting as an experienced gardener. But I knew the first day's work would be buddleja pruning. I looked it up in Dr D G Hessayon's *The Flowering Shrub Expert* ('cut back last year's growth to within 3–4 inches of the old wood'); Peter McHoy's *Pruning: A Practical Guide* ('in a small garden buddlejas are best cut back close to the ground each spring'); and the Royal Horticultural Society's *Pruning & Training* ('cut back all remaining stems to within two or three pairs of buds'). Thus armed, I turned pro.

The door was opened by a woman who had spent less time preparing for the moment than I had. In fact, she seemed to have forgotten I was coming. We established that I was Ben Dark: Gardener, while she rushed around looking for keys, cheerfully explaining that she had to head out. 'But there's the buddleja, the kids love it but we can barely see out of the kitchen window. It needs a good old tidy-up.' Once I was finished pruning, I was to make a start on the weeding and let myself out. She gave me twenty pounds and left.

Our tutors taught us pruning by the book. We were instructed to step back and look at the tree between each cut. Alone in the garden I did just that, snipping a branch and trudging over to the shed, then to the opposite corner to see things from that perspective. From the beginning it never seemed right, always appearing hacked at and too obviously pruned. I tried to reduce the cut stumps to balance things out, but this just made fatter and shorter stumps. Eventually all that remained was a stocky 'Y'-shape – something I could have made with two cuts from a pruning saw.

I still think of that woman and her buddleja-loving family. Did they laugh about the young man who came round and extolled the importance of pruning to three sets of buds, then chopped down the tree and ran away? She never phoned to ask when I was coming back. I'm saved from unendurable shame by knowing that four months after I had departed, they would have been given the buddleja show of their lives – huge panicles of flower, impossible to associate with the ropey old shrub they had once grown, drowning the garden in summer scent, while from the kitchen window the joyful children watched butterfly after butterfly jig across the glass.

There is a butterfly called the Camberwell Beauty, a rare visitor to the UK, named in 1748 for the parish in which it was caught. *Nymphalis antiopa* has not returned to London since, but it does occasionally set down in other parts, letting publications like *The Entomologist's Record and Journal of Variation* write softcore headlines such as 'Camberwell Beauties in the Isle of Man'. For Vladimir Nabokov, the Camberwell Beauty was young love. In *Speak, Memory* his trysts with Tamara begin in August as velvet-black Camberwell Beauties sail through the glades. As the year advances the pair become butterfly-like themselves, flitting to secret spots in the woods, tracked by Nabokov's voyeuristic tutor and his antique telescope. But then comes winter and a frigid spring. Tamara swaps her black hairband for a white hat. The Camberwell Beauty emerges bruised and bleached by hibernation. It has lived less than a year and yet it is ancient and soon to die. Two pages later, the memoir sheds Tamara and introduces Lenin.

Happily, Camberwell has picked the teenage sex version of the butterfly as its emblem. Turn right out of Grove Park, left on Church Street, straight over at the lights and on past the bus depot and you will find yourself under another railway bridge. The butterfly painted on the brickwork is a Camberwell Beauty in all the blue-spotted plushness of youth. Were Mary Poppins to glide along, snap her fingers and bring the thing to life, it would find itself in a strange urban heaven, only needing to follow the tracks past Denmark Hill Station to reach the nectar-rich buddlejas of Grove Park.

On a still day in early July, I found half-a-dozen Small Tortoiseshells feeding on the King Buddleja at No.104, making little up and down flutters between the florets as if just learning to fly. The pavement smelled of honey. To us the scent of buddleja is a reason to stop and sniff the air, a reminder of summer afternoons spent with suitcases at unmanned railway stations. To a butterfly it is the promise of succour. If the smell of Grove Park's King Buddleja were made suddenly visible, it would look like a smoke plume, flowing up and away like clouds from a chimney, at first distinct and almost solid, then breaking up into a morse code of fume and sky, and finally becoming diffuse, just another invisible component of the complicated air.

Tiny dissipated wafts of aromatic compounds have been shown to cause antenna twitch in laboratory butterflies and it is likely that chemicals on the breeze tell Lepidoptera at least as much about the world as their UV-saturated vision. The King Buddleja of Grove Park was producing vast quantities of at least thirty-three separate biosynthetic smells, the greatest of which was 4-oxoisophorone. When this molecule was isolated and taken to the World Perfumery Congress at Miami Beach, it was described as having notes that were variously sweet, honey, woody and musty. Others identified the complex smells of tobacco and saffron. To me saffron smells like warm hay, and rolling tobacco is early-morning reading for almost-due essays, but I am sad to say that loitering outside No.104 all I picked up was a strong floral aroma.

Butterflies don't have memory in the human sense. The six Small Tortoiseshells might visit King Buddleja on every sunny day from June to October, but they need to be attracted afresh each time. They do not sit in the dark planning meals like a gourmand on the Eurostar to Paris. They take flight each morning into a world that is as good as new, which means that as long as the King Buddleja has seeds to fertilize, it must produce its nectar bribe and the trail of sweet London air that advertises it. And my goodness what a lot of seeds there are. A shrub as large as this might produce upwards of three million. Most of these will fall on the road, the railway or the neighbouring plots. There they become part of the seedbank, that wonderful collection of potential plants found in every bed, border and windowbox. When Sir Edward Salisbury grew iron grass from under the pews, he was breaking open his church's unique seedbank, and when I let a lawn grow out in to a flowering meadow, I am drawing from another seedbank, one in which I hope pyramid orchids, ox-eye daisies and wild carrot have already been deposited.

Grove Park has its own seedbank, as individual as a thumb print. It would be possible to develop a garden from this alone. The ground would need to be rendered utterly bare before things were allowed to grow where they sprung. Weeding-out would be allowed, but no intentional planting or transplanting. The first few years would be easy. Here there would be poppies and centranthus and masses of dandelions and verbena. The problem would come when one grew bored of bright weeds and yearned for a bit of structure and shade. Trees would be required, some sturdier shrubs and maybe a hedge. What if the seeds fell in the wrong place? We could wait fifteen years for a yew seedling to make its way in, something to shape and pass on to the grandchildren as a vast topiary peacock, and then find it sprouting outside the front door. What choice but to step around it for forty years? One thing would be certain though: the Grove Park Seedbank Garden would always be full of buddleja.

It may be that the superabundance of buddleja on uncultivated ground is a bad thing. They are nectar-rich and good for flying pollinators, but they evolved alongside the insects of Sichuan Province and are thus almost invisible to our own terrestrial invertebrates. However, some do manage to feed. On Grove Park the King Buddleja is clean but its brother in the mossy pot at No.77 has a thick band of black aphids below its wilting tip. This seems backwards. An aphid is little more than a spike and a stomach; they don't suck from the plant, they tap in and swell. Healthy plants have more sap and more sugar and should be more appealing but it is the weak that are targeted. The perfume on the pavement tells us why: the King Buddleja is rich in chemical compounds. It is likely releasing biosynthetic aphid-repelling molecules. Many plants use this trick as a response to attack, though it has not yet been studied in the butterfly bush. Some plants even send out scent signals to predators, letting them know that upwind there are soft insect bodies for the eating. The poor weedy buddleja is barely able to keep from crossing the line between stem and stick, it does not have the resources for chemical warfare and so becomes aphid food.

We should be thankful for the sacrifice. Aphids are the krill of the front garden; everybody feeds on them, from sparrows, blackcaps and blue tits to lacewings, ladybirds and velvet mites. Yes, buddleja are not nearly so useful for wildlife as an endemic species might be, but they are better than a fence post. A large native oak might support two thousand three hundred species, a buddleja just thirty. This, of course, is an excellent argument for preserving mature oaks, wherever they may grow. They do not grow in South London chimney pots, however.

The naturalist and broadcaster L H Newman thought the Camberwell Beauty's name a great disappointment, 'for there is nothing pretty or rural about Camberwell now'. I disagree. Were he not long dead, I would invite Mr Newman to meet me on the bridge where Chadwick Road ends. On an early July evening, we would stand together in clouds of 4-oxoisophorone, until the 21:14 train from London Bridge swept south below us and night fell. There we would lean against the parapet and watch as all the nocturnal moths of Peckham and New Cross found their way to Grove Park's lone white buddleja.

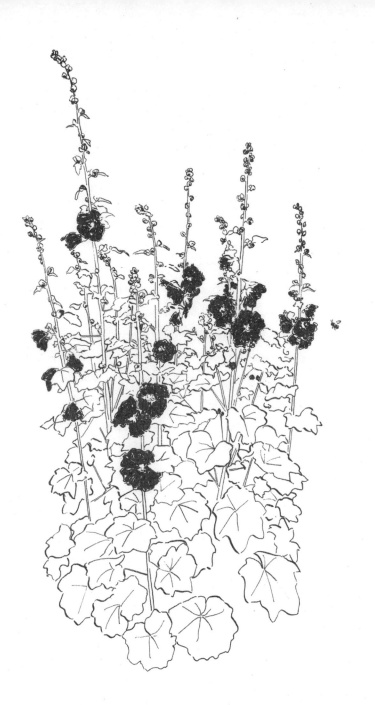

# 4

## HOLLYHOCK

On a hot cloudy day I walked to Grove Park with Solomon.
He was asleep, the humid air having knocked him into a shiny-faced coma. The only person around was a middle-aged man
who sat on a wall drinking cream soda from a pink can. He
stopped us to ask what time it gets dark in August. It was mid-July, but his question made sense: the mood on the road *was*
pure August.

In the borough of Southwark, blue bins are for recycling,
green bins are for rubbish and brown bins are for garden
waste. Beyond the man and his fizzy drink, the brown bins
were full, their lids propped up on the vegetation below.
One spilled strands of wisteria, long past flowering, another
swags of dusty ivy. After January, when the Christmas trees

are dismembered, midsummer is the busiest time of year for green waste collection. People go mad, or get bored, or both, and start hacking at shrubs. I was looking at severed pieces from the gardens behind the houses – the secret worlds that I cannot write about and have never visited, but that are probably 80 per cent of any Grove Park resident's gardening life.

The cut branches were a sign of the dog days. It is easy to lose patience with a garden that looked impossibly perfect three week ago but now seems to have given up. Grass dulls, leaves lose their shine and the very soil becomes matt and lifeless. What was so recently blue-bright and shimmering is flat and brown; a festival field at 9am, with work tomorrow and the car park calling; or a hairstyle that was amazing in the taxi but flat in the nightclub. The peonies are blown, the lilacs gone to seed. The forsythia, which flowered yellow when the trees were bare, outshining even the daffodils, has been forgotten. For too long it has been in its summer guise: messy, not quite upright, branches hung with tired leaves. When the homeowner slumps out with a sweaty back and pair of ratchet loppers, determined to do something (anything!) about the depressing state of it all, the forsythia is the first to go.

But there was still colour at No.92. Eight feet of it, with crimson flowers on leaning spires. These were hollyhocks

(*Alcea rosea*), serotonin for the summer soul. They were flowering in one of the Grove's true cottage gardens, behind a picket fence with little gates that had been conscientiously closed. A blue plumbago grew from a terracotta pot. Nearby there were lavenders, a shrubby hibiscus, white-flowered comfrey and a dark red sunflower of the best kind. Here was an antidote to the 'flowering gap', the cause of the horticultural malaise. Do away with spectacular massed plantings of things that bloom and fade, and settle instead for a pinch of everything, and two pinches of hollyhock for the sheer joy of it.

The burgundy form at No.92 seemed to be the endemic variety of this little corner of the Grove. A piece of collectively owned beauty, available to anyone who kept a scrap of soil and did not weed out every crinkly seedling that appeared. It grew tallest at No.88, its top flowers reaching the white lintel beam and showing like beads of blood. It was in the tree pit outside No.98, and leaned out between the flower pots at 99, blooming by the pretty little olive tree in that sunny square. It stood most abundantly at the front of 97's garden, doing an important job of looking interesting while the honey spurge faded and the Michaelmas daisies worked towards spangling themselves with blue stars.

No.97 is the street's most honourable garden. It has no wall, fence or railings and is fronted by a drop kerb and a double yellow line, clues that it was once a parking space. At some point the car was banished and its place given to a spreading, multi-stemmed cornus. It sits in a wonderful gravel garden with Mexican feather grass, snowdrops and the giant glaucous leaves of *Melianthus major*. What was once two hundred square feet of sterile paving, convenient for one family, had been transformed into a space that gave pleasure to anyone walking by. This was a noble act for which the communal hollyhock was surely some reward.

Dark red might be the default colour of Grove Park hollyhocks, but it needn't have been this way. Four back gardens away, on Grove Hill Road, a street that could easily be the subject of its own book, full of eccentric monkey puzzles, white iceberg roses and multi-headed cordylines, a shampoo-pink variety is dominant – more fresh but less exotic. As with those on Grove Park, it likes to grow as close to humans as possible and seems happiest where it can stretch out a large, ragged leaf and touch the front step. It is reminiscent of the nicest sort of cat: not dependent on its owner, but showing her affection in the sunny spots where their paths cross.

Qun Li, a botanist from Shenyang Agricultural University in China, has observed that the honey bee (*Apis mellifera*) is the most efficient distributor of hollyhock pollen. Perhaps this is true in Liaoning Province, on the northern shore of the Yellow Sea, where hollyhocks grow thick and wild across the Central Planes, but I have never seen one visit the Grove Park specimens. These are the sole preserve of the genus *Bombus*, the bumblebees. I'm sure if we had more hollyhocks, the honey bees would include them on their rounds. There are hives nearby and I see the workers out foraging. For years there was a colony on the flat roof of a kitchen extension in Ivanhoe Road, just a fence hop away. Their keeper used to climb out of a window by his upstairs toilet to attend them, until he moved to Nunhead and a garden by the great ruined cemetery. There he produced jars of 'graveyard honey', supposedly from the wild flowers and lime trees that grew between the tombs, but we both knew his bees spent their days in the garden centre down the road. They could still reach Grove Park – it is only about half a mile away, well within their flight zone – but they seemed happy to stick with their lorry-loads of Dutch zinnias and leave the hollyhocks to the bumblebees.

And how nice that they do. A buff-tailed *Bombus terrestris* beetling about in a hollyhock flower is one of the great comic sights of the English garden. It's the fat bottom that does it; they are always getting close to being wedged in as they try to reach the nectaries. Hollyhocks have a monadelphous androecium, that is, the filaments of their stamens are all fused together into an elongated tube with just the anthers protruding. Think of a classic hibiscus-print Hawaiian shirt; the suggestive nubbin that curves up from the flower's heart is a monadelphous androecium. In hollyhocks it is shorter and stouter than in hibiscus, perfect for half-trapping the broad-beamed insects while they rumble around in the pollen, looking and sounding like tiny brown bears trapped in the sugar store.

Dr Lettsom of Grove Hill knew the joy of looking at bees. In his pamphlet of 1796, *Hints for Promoting a Bee Society*, he very correctly observed that their 'active exertion is pleasing to contemplate, and the product of it profitable to enjoy'. He wanted every Londoner with the space for a hive to become a patron of the bee, and envisioned fifty thousand hives in the nurseries and market gardens that surrounded the Georgian metropolis. Lettsom questioned why so much energy was expended on exploiting distant colonial possessions while the abundance of the capital itself was left untapped. Bees would bring a little luxury into the poorest of houses and, Lettsom pointed out, honey could be spread on bread to save butter.

Henry Phillips takes up the idea in his *Flora Historica*, published over three volumes in 1829. In his chapter on hollyhocks he suggests bees as a primitive method of wealth distribution, writing, 'these industrious insects have peculiar claims on the care of the peasantry, since they stray into the grounds of the wealthy, where, without committing devastation or fraud, they obtain treasure for their master'. Phillips envisions a future where serf and lord alike are enriched by hollyhocks. They will grow at the edges of fields and hide every ugly fence and overgrown hedge in England. Here they will be food for the bees of the poor and the eyes of the rich. Alas, Phillips mourns, it will not be possible until 'the children of the lower classes of society are become more civilized...so that their amusement may not consist in idly destroying what cannot benefit them.'

I believe Phillips' idle destruction is a reference to the charming pursuit of making hollyhock dolls. Here's how. Take one fully unfurled flower and place it flared side down on a table. A small section of stalk should protrude from the green sepals at the base of the flower. Take another bud from slightly higher on the same spire, this one with petals that show colour but are still wrapped tight. It should be reminiscent of a whipped ice-cream's tip, blackcurrant if one is using Grove Park hollyhocks, raspberry for Grove Hill's. Strip away all the green from the bottom and five little holes will be exposed; these are the nectaries that the bumblebees are searching for, but seen from the other side. Slot the stalk from the first flower into one of these holes and you have a beautiful ballerina with a ruffled skirt, a little white face and high pink hair like a Marie Antoinette Barbie.

No matter what Henry Phillips might have thought, this was never a working-class pursuit, but a glorious trick to amuse all imaginative little boys and girls. Christopher Lloyd writes of making hollyhock fairies with his sister, and he grew up in an Arts and Crafts manor house.

I grew up in the Hampshire village of Sheet. Horticulturally, its most obvious feature was the vast horse chestnut on the village green. It was unmissable, cartoonishly big between the pub, the church and the village hall. But better than the tree were the hollyhocks. They grew, year after year, from the base of a much-repaired eighteenth-century wall, a mashup of brick, stone and crumbling mortar that stretched from the heart of the village down to the A272. The flowers, some growing ten feet tall, nearly as high as the wall itself, were all rooted in tiny strips of soil between the brick buttresses, where the tarmac of the road could not reach. All shades of pink were there, from raspberry juice to piglet skin, as well as lemon meringue and apricot. Despite this abundance on my doorstep, I have no memory of ever making a hollyhock doll, or seeing one put together by other children, so it seems the countryside may finally be safe and we can begin the long-postponed work of hiding every railing behind floral spires.

I won't call for a hollyhock revival, but only because that would be too much of a cliché. For two hundred years, we hacks have been demanding a reappraisal of these 'old-fashioned plants'. In 1836 *The Saturday Magazine* was already hoping that 'those possessed of taste will not reject the hollyhock because it so familiarly flourishes in the rustic gardens of the cottagers'. In 1870 Mr Fish, a correspondent for *The Field* ('The Country Gentleman's Newspaper'), reported with regret that he had 'lately seen some large gardens without a hollyhock at all' and hoped that with his pen he 'could give this grand old plant a fresh start'. Twenty years later nothing had changed, with *The Garden* using identical language when calling for a revival of this 'grand old plant'. Even garden designer and writer Gertrude Jekyll, writing for *Country Life* in 1911, could not avoid using 'grand' and 'old' to describe the flower, so thoroughly are they stuck to the plant.

Jekyll was writing in troubled times. A vicious disease, mallow rust (*Puccinia malvacearum*), had struck the hollyhock and was everywhere attacking them. The fungal infection causes yellow spots that mature into disfiguring black pustules.

Jekyll's recommendation was to spray with permanganate of potash and plant hollyhocks in at least a foot of good manure, though eighteen inches would be better. This rich diet was universally recommended for hollyhocks in the nineteenth and twentieth centuries, with Mr Fish of *The Field* blustering: 'You want hollyhocks eight feet high? Very well, give them a rich loam four foot deep, mixed with one fourth part of well-rotted farmyard manure.' And, as if this was not enough, they should be watered each week with liquid sewage. *The Garden* in 1891 recommends a sort of farmyard lasagne: a trench two feet deep, with a solid layer of manure at the bottom, then soil for nine inches, then manure, then a little more soil, before adding a topping of decayed manure. *Gardens Illustrated*, 1883, plumps for shaping one's ground into a manure-filled basin, the sides of which 'will collect the moisture that falls from the clouds'.

It is all madness. The hollyhocks of Sheet required no water and certainly no manure. They grew in the footings of the wall and the dust that blew off the asphalt. Self-seeding themselves every year with the only intervention being a few hand-painted signs saying 'Do Not Spray!'. The hollyhocks of Grove Park were treated just as meanly. There is no room for three feet of well-turned loam and an extra foot of manure next to the fibreoptic broadband cables and lamppost cement of an urban tree pit.

But we grow a different plant from Miss Jekyll, Mr Fish and Henry Phillips. Their hollyhocks were to stand in massed ranks, like plump young soldiers off to fight their very first battle. Our hollyhocks are loners, cowboys made thin on a diet of cheroots and redeye, more given to leaning on the saloon wall than standing straight on the parade ground. The Victorians took their hollyhocks clumped and ruffled, twenty flowers out at once, each of them five inches across. These are the plants that Vita Sackville-West rails against when she writes of the plants of her youth, all superbly grown and yet so displeasing to the modern taste: the lumps of galega, the vast delphiniums, the towering hollyhocks. She imagined the old gardener brought back to life – would he be hurt, horrified and offended by the informal muddle she made of her garden?

A good look dies hard and massed hollyhocks continued to be planted well into the twentieth century. There is a wonderful picture of the garden at Lambeth Palace, taken in 1934 or '35. The gardeners have ignored Miss Jekyll's advice to plant at the back of the border and have used their hollyhocks as bedding, taking them right to the edge of a curving grass path. The hollyhock has a human aura – it is vaguely person-sized with big round flowers like eyes; the effect at the Palace was of a massed crowd, gathered on the streets of some medieval city to welcome a hero or jeer a criminal. Even in black and white, the image is spectacular, in person it must have been awe-inspiring.

We will never know if the Palace's resident at the time, the Most Reverend Cosmo Lang, Archbishop of Canterbury, requested the hollyhocks or had them thrust upon him. Being head gardener at a grace-and-favour residence is a unique and challenging job. You remain, the outline of the garden stays immutable, but the people occupying the house leave every few years, taking their tastes, preoccupations, must-haves and banned plants with them. Imagine the next Archbishop, William Temple, coming in to meet the staff and saying, 'Now lads, two things about me: I love God and I hate hollyhocks.' Everything would change in an afternoon.

But is that really likely? Does anyone hate hollyhocks? They do die back rather messily. This was not a problem for the Victorians, who cut them to the ground as soon as flowering was finished, but it can be for those of us who grow them hard and let them seed. In November they are tall grey skeletons, looming in the mists, a reminder of summer long gone. This is surely why Tennyson chose them for his mournful song of the autumn garden, 'A Spirit Haunts the Year's Last Hours':

Heavily hangs the broad sunflower
Over its grave i' the earth so chilly;
Heavily hangs the hollyhock,
Heavily hangs the tiger-lily.

When the clocks go back at the end of October it is suddenly dark on my cycle home. The shift takes people by surprise and catches them with their lights on and their curtains open. This is particularly true for people working in home offices. I understand why. It feels seedy and unrewarding to get up, close the curtains and go back to the computer for another tranche of emails. Curtain closing is a job for the end of the day when the employee dies and the private self is reborn.

I've struck up a voyeuristic relationship with a man in the Chiltern Hills. I glimpse him with his back to the window as I speed down to the station and my train back to London. He has short greying hair and his room is lit up cold and blue by two flatscreen monitors. Sometimes he's looking at a chart, but mostly it's a spreadsheet or an email inbox. The wall he faces is incongruously covered in bright hollyhock wallpaper. Every time he looks up he must see floral spires. For four years he has been at the desk. By now he has probably spent more time looking at hollyhocks than Gertrude Jekyll and Mr Fish combined, and yet no hollyhocks grow in his garden.

To return to a long-unanswered question, in August it gets dark at 8.30pm, well after the working day has finished and the computers have been shut down. I would like to throw some hollyhock seeds into this man's garden and let him wash the working day from his eyes with the spreadsheet's living antithesis: the pollen-dusted bottom of a nectar-drunk bumblebee.

# 5

# RED VALERIAN

On a narrow road near Grove Park is a gravelled garden with five wheelie bins and two lime trees (*Tilia × europaea*). A high privet hedge keeps it from the neighbours to the left and nothing but daffodils and lavender separate it from those on the right.

The daffodils are *Narcissus* 'Geranium', three heads to a stem, with orange cups and warm white petals. In March and April they are the best thing on the street, flowering in their hundreds and rolling the smell of crushed laurel over pavements. In February they look promising and in May and June they are appalling, enough to make one question if daffodils should be allowed to grow in London. They flop onto the paths, get trodden on, have bins wheeled over them, crisp up and sink back to the depths, as thankful to go as we are to see them leave. The lavenders flower on alone.

It is a jolly and well-intentioned sort of space, particularly in its seven-week prime, but hardly one of the world's great shows. No one ever stops to take a picture. I know this because, as you have probably guessed, behind the bins and the bay window I sit writing this book.

If I may make a case for my defence, the growing space is no-man's land. There are three flats in our house, the same next door. The strip of flower bed is thus shared by around fifteen people, each with some right to fill it with their own favourite plants, a right that had never been exercised until we moved in. There are similar multi-occupancy houses up on the Grove. They have the same plethora of bins and the same planting inertia. My daffodils can't help. All I can do is give the wind seeds and hope they drift true. To this end, I have introduced a new plant to Grove Park.

This might be a sin. There is a horticultural legend that has Ellen Willmott (1858–1934), the stately gardener of Warley Place – grower of *Narcissus*, winner of medals and spender of fortunes – scattering seeds unbidden into the gardens of her friends and rivals. By these actions, it is said, the giant sea holly (*Eryngium giganteum*) acquired its common name: Miss

Willmott's ghost. It somehow doesn't ring true. In flower, the plant is a beauty, a candelabra of blue thistle-cones, each rising from a spiny collar of silver bracts. I suspect Ellen Willmott was a proselytizer, a sea holly evangelist with the influence to see it planted in any spot she half-suggested. Strewing another's border with unwanted seed is an act of vandalism. It is impolite, offensive even. Willmott's reputation was that of a 'difficult woman', which is to say, an 'ambitious woman'. She was not afraid to argue but she took horticulture seriously and would not do anything as base and underhand as introducing a species without consent. Unless...unless she thought she was helping people who for some reason could not help themselves.

My ghost is crimson. It is red valerian (*Centranthus ruber*), a memory maker, the kind of plant that lodges in the brain. It will grow in crushed brick and sea salt, defiant of drought, thriving on neglect. And yet its leaves are glossy and its flowers abundant. There is nothing of the wire-and-dust survivor about it. It is a portion of stately home herbaceous border that has been scooped up and plastered onto a cracked chimney or a sun-blasted rockface. Its buds open cough-drop bright and fade to raspberry on a long spire like a thyrse of lilac stretched thin by pulling. It is technically a subshrub, but if cut back in November, it will spend winter as a neat rosette of salad greens.

At work we grow it in a set of ruined urns in half-shade under an oak tree. It leans out towards the light, growing up, then out and then up again, as if blown from the woods on a breeze. A few of its earliest flowers we allow to seed. The capsules resemble the sabella worms that build tubes of mud on the seabed and poke fans out to sift the current. It is a seed that parachutes on its fronds, too heavy to fly but light enough to fall sideways. It finds its way into unpromising cracks and there germinates. Sometimes, after setting root, it is winkled out and shipped to Camberwell in a gardener's lunchbox.

In his brilliant garden-diary-and-so-much-more, *Modern Nature*, Derek Jarman recalls his childhood on the Oxfordshire airbase his father commanded. Derek is briefly entrusted to Jonno, a delinquent youth on National Service, prime example of Wing Commander Lancelot Jarman's talent for choosing his most unsuitable recruits to serve as babysitters. Jonno is a Ton-Up Boy, one of the proto-rockers named for biking at over a hundred miles an hour. He has the lining of his trouser pockets cut out and makes little Derek stick his hands through as they roar on a motorcycle past the bleak military houses, their mown lawns divided by barbed wire, their rockeries built from air-raid shelters, to the bombed-out house where a riot of red valerian draws bees and butterflies to the ruins. This is the gateway to the wild; to the chestnuts, the cuckoopint, the celandine and the snowdrops, everything that did not grow and was not wanted in the bleak gardens of the Royal Air Force's married quarters.

I wonder if Derek Jarman thought of those awful, thrilling rides when he slouched past the red valerian in his garden at Prospect Cottage in Dungeness. How could he not? It is a plant uniquely able to bring back time and place. It loves the unloved places, the almost-gardens, the edges of towns, the spaces that call to people who need time away from people. My own defining memory of *Centranthus ruber* is more prosaic and comes with the unromantic National Trust logo attached. One ceaseless summer in my very early twenties, I went down to Ightham Mote in Kent. Heat had cooked away the birds and bleached the grass. Not a drop of rain had fallen in six weeks but the sloping stone walls of the moat blazed with ruby red valerian. It was a useful reminder for an early career gardener who had become obsessed with 'improving the soil': you can break blooms from the thinnest ground.

This was a lesson I could have learned closer to home. On Grove Park, local residents have jemmied tough species into the tree pits. The growing is hard. Each rectangle allows space only for the plane tree's roots and trunk, leaving the other plants to fight for the scraps available to them. On a recent walk through the Grove I found snowdrops, sedums, wallflowers, hardy geraniums, rose campions, mullein, yew, calendula, hollyhocks, buddleja, tree echiums, hellebores, Welsh poppies, Mexican fleabane, iris, liriope, thyme, pansies and nasturtiums growing in the little rectangles. And even clematis, honeysuckle and climbing roses. Mediterranean spurge (*Euphorbia characias* subsp. *wulfenii*) grew in one pit, lighting the afternoon phosphoric green. From the pit its seeds had hopped the pavement into an uncultivated garden where new plants provided a miraculous distraction from the bins and the concrete they stood on. It was doing the work I hope my red valerian will one day assist in.

The garden designer Dan Pearson, once a native of this patch, writes beautifully on the interconnected nature of city gardens. His *Home Ground: Sanctuary in the City* is about a fenced plot in crowded Southeast London. From his window he looks down on nearby gardens; this one newly tenanted and sporting its first beard of creeping thistle, that one a hoary veteran of neglect, its hypothetical edges hidden under a canopy of semi-mature sycamore. Pearson likens the decades-long cycle of overgrowth and eventual clearing to the ancient practice of coppicing; some day the house with the self-sown sycamores will be sold and its trees will be levelled for a lawn and a trampoline, by then a neighbour three gardens removed will have turned his back on the world, shutting the curtains and giving up on the outside as the thistles creep back and shelter the tree seeds. The wildness is constant, it just shifts places.

But was my adding an opportunistic self-seeder to the vegetation that drifts and sloshes over this postcode the right thing to do? Perhaps not. Red valerian spreads. There are constant drives to eradicate it from seaside shale ecosystems. Volunteers for the Essex and Suffolk National Trust make yearly landings on Orford Ness and fight it on the beaches. The work parties are battling to keep threatened native plants such as yellow vetch (*Vicia lutea*), golden samphire (*Inula crithmoides*) and sea heath (*Frankenia laevis*) from being driven into the waves and lost forever. The speculation among the volunteers is that long ago red valerian escaped from the lighthouse keeper's garden. It is a bit of comforting prettiness gone utterly rampant. The lighthouse itself only managed two hundred and twenty-eight years. It was demolished in 2020 before shoreline erosion could send it splashing into Hollesley Bay. I suspect *Centranthus ruber* will prove a more lasting presence.

Perhaps the lonely keeper and his invasive plant was a warning to the governmental conservation body, English Nature, and influenced their attitude towards Prospect Cottage. In the mid-1990s they notified Keith Collins, partner of the by-then late Derek Jarman and keeper of his remarkable driftwood and seakale garden, that he had too much *Centranthus ruber*. Their letter made things very plain: 'do not gardenize'. But their intentions were noble; Prospect Cottage lies in a nature reserve that is at once a Special Protection Area (SPA), a Special Area of Conservation (SAC) and a Site of Special Scientific Interest (SSSI). Grove Park is none of these things. It is not a shale bank and its tree pits, with their pillars of hybrid plane (*Platanus × acerifolia*), are not fragile plant communities. They would never admit to it down at the art college, but Camberwell has been well and truly gardenized. I do not think my seedling will change the essential character of the area, and anyway, this is not red valerian's first visit to London.

*Centranthus ruber* came to us from the Mediterranean basin and has been growing in the South of England for over four hundred years. In *The English Gardener, or, A Sure Guide to Young Planters and Gardeners* of 1670, the nurseryman and author Leonard Meager lists the catalogue of flowers he grew beyond his vegetable beds. He considered red valerian 'fit for a Flower-pot', by which he meant suitable to bring into the house, still rooted and in full flower, a method of display more common in the seventeenth century than severing blooms from their stems and arranging them in vases.

The plant makes an even earlier appearance in British horticulture's most famous book, John Gerard's *Herball, or Generall Historie of Plantes*, published in 1597 and affectionately known as *Gerard's Herball*. The work describes hundreds of plants according to their appearance, habits, names and uses. At its heart it is a barely disguised translation of Rembert Dodoens' *Cruydeboeck* (herb book) with additional borrowings from Gerard's one-time friend and editor Matthias de l'Obel, as well as falsehoods, mistakes and lazy rumour-mongering, which are all the Englishman's own. The historian Charles E Raven finds it hard to acquit Gerard of 'almost all the sins of which a man of letters or of science can be guilty' but still acknowledges his enthusiasm, confidence and invigorating zeal.

Gerard would make a genuinely excellent gardening correspondent for any of today's newspapers. He might be botanically inept (God help anyone searching for gentians with the *Herball* as a guide) but he is warm, anecdotal, experimental and confessional; in short, a modern writer masquerading as an Elizabethan scholar. Take his entry on red valerian, which he said 'groweth plentifully' in his own garden: 'at the top of the stalks do grow very pleasant and long red flowers...which being past, the seeds are carried away with the wind...so that without great diligence the seed is not to be gathered or preserved: for myself have often endeavoured to see it, and yet have lost my labour.'

Red valerian sets seed in midsummer. The typical July day in London sees a westerly breeze of 9.9 miles per hour. It licks the buildings and lingers in the streets, soaking up smells and sliding them onwards. For this reason, the poor have always lived in the east of the city. An immortal observer, standing on the dome of St Paul's Cathedral from the day it was finished until the skyscrapers came and blocked the view, would have seen a hundred thousand days begin with sunrise over slums and finish with sunset over mansions, only the distances between them would have changed. Gerard wrote his *Herball* after the mass adoption of coal and before the installation of sewers. His was a stinking city and his monarch, Elizabeth I, chose to keep upwind in her preferred palace of Whitehall. Even so, at normal wind speed and direction, the breeze that took the seeds from John Gerard's centranthus would have blown over the Virgin Queen just seven minutes earlier.

I mention this only to further reassure myself that introducing red valerian to Grove Park was not an immoral action. Queen Elizabeth I died a tremendously long time ago, and red valerian was on the air even then. Gerard gardened in Holborn, an area of London that has been known for many things, but never for a surfeit of centranthus. The number of common names the plant has tells us something of how long it has been a part of British life. In James Britten and Robert Holland's 1886 work, *A Dictionary of English Plant-Names*, it is listed as pretty Betsy in Essex, scarlet lightning in Huntingdonshire, sweet Betsy in Kent and sweet Mary in Buckinghamshire. In Devon it is American lilac and bouncing bess, drunken sailor and Bovisand soldier. The white form is delicate Bess. It is cat bed in the Lincolnshire town of Kirton in Lindsey, and drunken Willies in Dunster down in Somerset. It has also been widely known as red cow basil, good neighbourhood, German lilac and fox's brush. All of these names represent the flowers' presence in the life of the locals, a significant enough part of day-to-day existence to warrant a nickname.

Truth be told, *Centranthus* was already on the Grove when I planted my seedling. A woody-stemmed specimen grew in the tree pit by No.37 and a smaller one by No.14. But they were both 'Albus', the white-flowered form, a plant I associate with flower beds and not rocky crevices. Associate is the word here.

For me, red *Centranthus ruber* conjures summer sun and the dust by the wall at Ightham Mote. *Centrathus ruber* 'Albus' is different. It reminds me of a shaded border, edged in unclipped box. It is overcast there, and always softly raining. Behind the low hedge are thin spikes of purple salvia and pink roses. In the watery light, the white of the flowers is perfect and the whole scene tastes faintly of peppermint, though none of the plants carry that fragrance. This is nowhere I have ever been and it is not somewhere I visit when I think of either purple salvia or pink roses. It is a little room in my brain accessed only when I think of delicate Bess.

The white flowers occur by themselves. *Centranthus ruber* is a polymorph, a plant whose natural populations have more than one form of appearance. Around one in ten plants have an instruction (or perhaps an obstruction) in their genetic code that halts or greatly scales back the production of anthocyanin – the red pigment responsible for autumn's colour and blackberry's stain. Our native foxglove (*Digitalis purpurea*) is another anthocyanin-dependent polymorph. It has four distinct forms: purple, pale purple, white with purple speckles, and pure white. These are not a blend of their parents' colours. Dark purple and white do not necessarily add up to pale purple. The plant's phenotype depends on dominant and recessive genes, like human eye colour. Two dark-flowered plants can produce a white-petalled seedling.

Just five per cent of the UK's yellow-flowered plants are polymorphic. In comparison, 24 per cent of the UK's pink- and red-flowered species are polymorphs. The common dandelion is a classic monomorph, capable of seeding itself into a million lawns without seeing a single petal fade. Clover flits between white and pink; celandine is yellow forever. Having two or more colours is a disadvantage in plants pollinated by insects. Bees often visit one species at a time and may not include a white-flowered specimen on their purple flight. But evolution is too efficient to let a damaging trait be widespread. Polymorphism *must* convey advantages or it would have died out. A recent study of anthocyanin-dependent polymorphs saw a number of specimens growing in both dry and well-watered conditions, including *Holcus lanatus*, the soft-flowered grass known as Yorkshire fog; *Persicaria maculosa*, the weed of disturbed ground on which I learned to use an Austrian scythe; *Vicia sepium*, a bush vetch; *Cirsium palustre*, the seven-foot marsh thistle; and *Digitalis purpurea*, the foxglove. In the drought beds, the pink forms of every species produced more seeds than their white counterparts. In the irrigated field, the white form far outperformed the pink.

We can speculate that anthocyanin is used by the plants to form flavonoids, which, in their turn, absorb damaging free radicals produced by a plant trying to grow in stressful conditions. But the main point is: a tree pit needs the red form of *Centranthus ruber* if it is going to produce enough seed to turn the few wastelands on Grove Park into evocative edge spaces. My seedling is growing in a tree pit by No.104. One day I would like to visit and see that it has made it over the wall and into the grid of slabs. I hope that someone has the best years of their life behind that front door, and that when they are retired, out in the countryside somewhere, well past living in a flat in Camberwell, they see red valerian and remember the ugly bins and beautiful plant that grew round them, the smell of the summer and people they knew long ago.

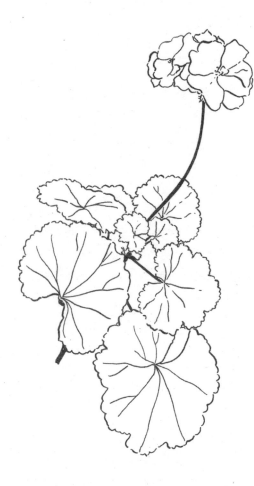

# 6

## PELARGONIUM

On a Wednesday in August, it rained hard, the kind of weather that plasters clothes to bodies, runs down legs, soaks socks inside their shoes and bubbles from boot holes. For three hours, the sky was dark and the mood autumnal. At 6pm it stopped and the waste of all that wet became clear. This remained a summer city. The pavements were still hot, the roads steamed. The cars and the kerbs all radiated. Up it came. London was an overclocked reactor core, hissing under the hoses, looking to meltdown.

I had been soaked and shivering when I left the Chilterns, but in a dry T-shirt I walked the Grove in a hug of warmth, the feeling of a soft jumper after a cold swim. Solomon was not so content. He was eight months old now and teething. His cot had become an overheated and uncomfortable place and we drifted the streets in search of sleep. Dusk fell on our slow way up Grove Park, as all the plants of the familiar gardens were losing their colours and becoming shapes. At No.30, a planter of orange pelargoniums flickered in the dark.

The pelargonium is a familiar plant from South Africa, widely and wrongly known as the geranium. Pelargoniums are generally frost-tender with fleshy upright stems; hardy geraniums tend to be herbaceous mounds of leaf that die back in winter. The two genera were separated in 1789 by Charles Louis l'Héritier de Brutelle, a botanist about whom Sir Joseph Banks, English botanist and explorer, wrote: '...of all the impudent Frenchmen in the whole world he is the most impertinent & dangerous'. The provocation had been a letter from l'Héritier explaining that he was in Britain on the run from the Spanish and French governments, having liberated a tranche of newly collected botanical specimens, and that he had put them through customs under Banks's name. The Frenchman then arrived at Sir Joseph's door and stayed for fifteen months. He used the great man's herbarium to research his *Geraniologia*.

L'Héritier was a wealthy obsessive. It was said that he spent twenty thousand francs a year on botany and walked between appointments to save on a carriage. He survived the French Revolution but was murdered, some say assassinated, on one of those walks on a similarly hot August night in 1800. Two centuries later and the name change he instigated simply will not stick. Pelargoniums and geraniums remain hopelessly tangled in the shared brain of the gardening public. Perhaps they will stay that way forever.

The little plants are like soldiers: often charming as individuals and very bad news en masse. The Victorians planted them in brigades and battalions, fifteen thousand identical plants strong, the musk of empire hovering all about them. They were red-coated infantry, set to march over parks and gardens, claiming the wild soil in the name of flower beds and 'a damn good show'. This bedding was made and unmade each year. It has mostly gone now. There is neither the labour nor the appetite for it in modern gardens. The greenhouses where the tender young plants were sown and struck have been sold off and smashed down and, for a hundred and thirty years, the horticultural cognoscenti have been fighting a war against the floral mosaic, though their opponent was mortally wounded in 1910 and has been dying in a public park ever since.

The great writer and plantsman E A Bowles, a friend of Gertrude Jekyll and a connoisseur of wild snowdrops, once visited a friend whose borders were long ribbons of bedding flowers (receding to infinity like Macbeth's kings). Bowles suggested that his gardeners might just as well paint the ground and brush the snow off when needed. This dismissive attitude to massed pelargoniums has prevailed. There is no art in the obvious. We are happy when a garden designer talks about planting in brushstrokes but would be revolted if they began to talk of flowers used as pixels. Then it all gets a bit Legoland. Pockets of carpet bedding do survive, however. They can be found outside municipal buildings in county towns; in the Great Fountain Garden at Hampton Court; at the seaside, Eastbourne is best; in Edinburgh's immaculate Princes Street Gardens; at Waddesdon Manor in Buckinghamshire; and Lyme Park in Cheshire. All places that glory in anachronism, either in the name of heritage or by plain inclination. Unless there is a royal wedding or a jubilee, bedding is only planted in places it has always been.

As a young man I set pelargoniums in the Italian Garden at Chiswick House. They were grown from September cuttings, sheltered all winter from the winds and cold. Trowelling them into the urns and parterre beds felt significant. I was summer's priest, relighting the temple flame from a wick kept smouldering in the desert.

Horticultural work always comes untucked and gardens are never finished. I left Chiswick with the grounds needing as much work as the day I arrived. Over three centuries, scores of gardeners had worked the sixty-five acres, and each of us left bittercress and brambles for our successor. A great garden is a cross-generational endeavour, but it is *not* a cathedral. We are not stonemasons and there is no bishop to daub our finished work with holy oil. We are eternal plate-spinners and literal mole-whackers, always struggling to keep *this* little piece of crust synced with notions of prettiness, forever tidying away nature. We are fish brushing sand from our rock, though tides and the whole Atlantic gyre work against us.

Of my ancestral gardeners at Chiswick, we know little. Charles Edmonds stewarded the grounds through peak geranium, serving as Head Gardener for forty years from 1838 to 1878. His obituary in *The Gardener's Chronicle* describes him as 'a safe and sound practitioner' and under his tenure visitors to Chiswick reported it crowded with glaziers and heating engineers, so we can guess he was a good hot-house man. But what of the gardeners who worked under him? Dynasties raised behind the camellias, sleeping in bunks like melons in their hammocks. Their names are inked in wage books but they are otherwise lost to us. Someone once told me that

Lord Burlington's original canal at Chiswick was dug by Cornishmen. 'You think Londoners could dig that?' he said, smiling at the water. 'Had to be Cornishmen.' But he was from Cornwall and I don't believe him.

We do know that by the mid-nineteenth century, the gardeners were growing pelargoniums. In his 1858 book *How to Lay Out a Garden*, Edward Kemp talks admiringly of a visit to Chiswick House where every path, even in the kitchen garden, was bounded by bright rows of scarlet geraniums and yellow calceolarias. When I pressed the plants into the soil of the Italian Garden, I honoured those forgotten gardeners. They tended their cuttings and February-sown seeds with pride, watched them rise like moss in March and worried about April's hardening off, a long greenhouse game of open-window-close-window. Those men gave their lives to something now regarded as vomitingly bad taste. But we should not pity them – some of us will share the same fate.

The pelargoniums of Grove Park belong to a different tradition, that of jewel-like clusters worn by buildings. A diamond brooch in contrast to carpet bedding's rhinestone jacket. They recall the effortless clash of scarlet petals and pale stone seen on the balconies of Paris. In South Africa, the pelargonium is a plant of the arid rock face and so it is perfect for wealthy Parisians. The *juillettistes* and *aoûtiens* can take their summer month in the country and come back to a plant that has thrived unwatered in their absence. They grow yet better in the South of France where they can seed and survive. In Toulouse, a few plants growing ragged on a wall led to a monk's conviction for murder. At 6am on the 16th of April 1847, a gravedigger found the body of a young girl in the St Aubin cemetery. Cécile Combettes lay in the right angle created by two joining walls. One separated the burial ground from a public street, the other kept it from the garden of a monastery. It had rained for days but there were no footprints in the soft soil and it was reasoned that Cécile had been thrown down from above. In the girl's loose hair, a single petal was found and matched to a plant on the monastery wall. The geranium was in almost perfect bloom but missed one petal. The investigation concluded that Cécile had met her end in the religious institution and Frère Léotade was sentenced for murder.

The evidence against the monk was scant and transcripts of the trial shed doubt on the verdict. Looking back with our gaze unclouded by anti-clerical sentiment (hard for some), it seems clear that the petal condemned a man of God and saved the killer, Cécile's master Bertrand Conte. But the pelargonium giveth and the pelargonium taketh away. In 1869 a worthy novel was published by an author with the sense to remain anonymous. In *Jenny's Geranium* we meet Mat Freeman, a violin-playing navvy and a giant of a man. With his head of flaxen hair, his blue shining eyes, ruddy cheeks and strong, clear voice, he is every urchin's dream of health and prosperity. But Mat has a secret. He was once a drunken wastrel, living in a dreadful hole with all the housekeeping money gone on gin, and his children dreading his stumbling returns. Until his wife brought home a little geranium and Mat found himself cleaning the window to give it light, which led to cleaning the room, which led to cleaning himself, eschewing the pub and going to church. Mat's geranium is now a venerable old thing, grandmother to many plants, one of which he has given to Jenny, a poor wretch living in the most disreputable alley in London.

The geranium is the only light in Jenny's miserable life and it is stolen by a drunk, her own father no less, who takes it to the bottle shop to sell for drink. The landlady likes pretty flowers. She shakes her curls and hisses, 'Pour that man a drop of gin.' But Mat bursts in shouting, 'NO YOU DON'T' with a voice like thunder, silencing the crowd and saving not only Jenny's geranium but the soul of her father and, indeed, the whole slum in which she lives, for the flower stirs a remembrance of better things in even the roughest and rudest men, and soon prayers and psalms are heard in the blighted streets. Nathaniel Bagshaw Ward, inventor of the glass Wardian case that protected exotic seedlings from salty sea air, and who thus birthed the intercontinental trade in live plants, wrote: 'The sight of a flower on a window-sill imparts a gleam of hope and of respect. It redeems the surrounding debasement. You feel that however hard the toil and poor the sustenance of the cultivator, the higher faculties of enjoyment and taste have not been ground away.'

If the idea of a man crashing into a pub and slamming a plant pot on the bar strikes us as ridiculous, we should examine the criminal records kept at the Old Bailey. Geranium theft was real and people paid dearly for it. In August 1884 Octavius Clark was transported to a penal colony for ten years for stealing 'eighteen plants called geraniums'. William Stone and Joseph Hanson were transported for seven years in 1829 for stealing geraniums, despite protesting that they bought them from a fishmonger whose whereabouts they had forgotten. The theft of a geranium in Pimlico saw Jane Eatherton transported for a similar stretch, and in 1858 Matthew Thurborn bought a geranium with counterfeit coin. As the police led him away, he handed the plant to a passing child, saying 'You may as well have this, for it will be no good to me now.' He was sentenced to twelve months hard labour and thus was proved correct – the pelargonium would never have survived the winter without him.

Pelargoniums do not die well. We cannot blame them. It is not a fault of temperament but of genetics. They evolved under an easterly wind from the Indian Ocean. The exotic parentage of those on Grove Park is hazy, but it is likely that they are a cross between *Pelargonium inquinans* and *Pelargonium zonale*. Both would expect to see out their days as a medium-sized shrub, somewhere between knee and nose height, depending on the soil. Under the southern skies of home they would be evergreen and live for years. Here they offer nothing to the polar vortices but their tender stems. They are innocent in the face of the first hard frost and are left with all their cells ice-blown and ruptured. Eurasian and North American plants would never be caught looking like twigs dipped in boiled spinach – it is a waste of good tissue. But the pelargonium does not drop its leaves and pump its sap full of anti-freezing sugars. No environmental trigger tells it to draw down into the soil and wait for better times. It is at the mercy of the gardener.

There was barbecue smoke on the air as the pram wheels thrummed Solomon to sleep. I walked to the end of the Grove and turned back. When I reached No.30 again the pelargoniums were lost in the gloom, just their pot visible as a black silhouette on the white windowsill. I gave them a two-in-three chance of survival. They were next to the house, they were dry under an overhanging lintel and they were in London, the hottest heat island in this warming archipelago. In the majority of winters, when our weather billows in fat, damp gusts from the west, they would live on. The other times would kill them, when the golden grasshopper on the Royal Exchange points east and we take on continental airs. On that August night I had no idea what their fate would be, but I'm writing this from the other side of winter and I'm afraid they did not make it. They saw Christmas and a month of the new year before February froze them solid in their pot.

They are dead now, but what a life they lived. Pelargoniums are people-pleasers, little pleasure machines bred to bring joy. In streets of shrub and shade they stand out like birthday balloons. Walter P Wright wrote *The Perfect Garden* in 1908 from the fashionable heart of the anti-bedding movement, and correctly identified the pelargonium as the heart and soul of the hated system. 'But,' he added, 'it is very hard to feel a whole-hearted detestation for a geranium. You might as well try to hate a sparrow...There is something irresistibly cheerful about both geraniums and sparrows.' Gertrude Jekyll worried that the plant's rise had irreversibly damaged the skill of the nation's gardeners. Still, she used them in her Arts and Crafts garden at Munstead Wood. Visitors would spot her over the globe thistles and irises of the summer border and rush up, panting, about the outmoded little flowers they had spotted. 'I should have thought that you would have despised geraniums,' they would say. 'On the contrary,' Gertrude would reply, 'I love geraniums. There are no plants to come near them for pot, or box, or stone basket.'

Pelargoniums are plants from the school of 'I'll have the thing that makes me most happy.' They were Charles Dickens' favourite flower. Mary 'Mamie' Dickens wrote of her father: 'He loved all flowers, but especially bright flowers, and scarlet geraniums were his favourite of all.' There is a photograph of him in the garden at Gad's Hill with his two living daughters. Dickens sits backwards on a wire chair. Kate stands behind with a hand on his shoulder, and Mary sits alongside, her chair hidden by her skirts. All three look at a book that Charles holds open. No doubt, before the photographer required him to hold his mouth shut for a minute or so, he had been reading to the little group. Behind them is the house and beneath its bay windows sits a geranium theatre. It is a steep terrace of shelves and blocks crowded with pots. These are not the flowers of one summer, they are as exuberant and vaguely directional as the writer's beard. They are kinked and branched. Although presented as a group, they are clearly individual plants. It is a system that combines the in-your-face mass of colour of the bedding programme with the petals-on-brickwork glory of a French tub. Even in black and white, the petalled domes are irresistible. They make one want to climb into the image, push over the satisfied author, dodge his doting children and make off into the lanes of Kent with a double armful of blooms. Such is the power of a pretty flower.

The horticultural world is full of obscure things that can be grown in specialist places. Plants that are unknown beyond a circle of connoisseurs, often for very good reason: they are ugly, they die when looked at, they are impossible to propagate or they grow forty feet in fifteen years. The windowsill geranium does no such thing. They welcome us home, smiling. They bring cheer to passing fathers and their almost-sleeping children. They can be bought in any supermarket and swapped for a swig of gin. Every house on Grove Park has a windowsill; it remains a mystery why they do not all hold a little pot of scarlet wonders.

# 7

## BOX

On the third day of September, I conducted an audit of the street's box plants (*Buxus sempervirens* and *Buxus microphylla*). My preparation was for a serious undertaking. I would be stopping at one house in four, comparing different uses of the topiarist's evergreen: neat freaks versus texture fiends, cubists versus ballers. It would be a study of hedges, I imagined, but there would also be stops beneath bay windows and views up the steps to door-flanking containers. I took a writing pad and set aside a few hours, but returned after just twenty minutes with five brief notes. There was more box growing inside my head than on the ground in Camberwell.

I once walked the Grove behind two teenagers carrying guitars. They had probably come from one of the houses.

One asked the other, 'Do you ever play with your dad?' 'Not really,' replied his friend, 'my dad's more into techno.' It was shocking. Dads aren't into techno, are they? Surely dads are into the Rolling Stones. But, of course, that's my dad, and dads have moved on. Gardens have too, but a part of me is stuck in the earlier years of my career when Tom Stuart-Smith was smashing the Chelsea Flower Show with cloud-pruned box, and *Buxus sempervirens* was *the* London plant.

I should have known there would be little box. UK horticulture watched it die for decades. Since the late 1990s, the little shrub had been under attack from *Cylindrocladium buxicola*, a fungus better known as box blight. It is likely that the pathogen had been feeding on a member of the *Buxus* genus for millennia, probably in some geographically isolated valley or mountain pass. But it found its way to this wet island, went forth and spectacularly multiplied.

*Cylindrocladium buxicola* reproduces asexually. A spore finds harbour on a leaf and geminates, pushing a tube through the tissue like a root through sand. It branches, and the branches branch, until it tangles into a threaded nest of mycelium, all of it releasing digestive enzymes, eating the plant from the inside. After three days of liquefaction and absorption, the fungus begins to emerge from stomata on the leaf's surface. Fertile branches secrete a viscous mucilage containing clusters of cylindrical spores, each one ready to wash or float away and start a new colony in a new plant or garden.

Microscopic box blight spores are probably not in my lungs as I write this, or in yours as you read it, though it's certainly possible. A strip of paper coated in Vaseline and placed in an infected border will generally pull some from the breeze, but in vanishingly small quantities compared to the mist of *Cladosporium* and *Aspergillus* mould we take in each day. For the main part, blight spores travel in water. Rain splashes them from plant to plant or they are washed into the mud and spattered back up. Sometimes they join a rivulet and flow free. In a nursery study, some of the highest concentrations of *Cylindrocladium* DNA were found in the drains.

An infected plant's terminal symptoms are root rot, stem lesions, canker, dieback and death, but it may also suffer episodes of leaf spot, wilt and defoliation. Attacks are managed with fungicide, good husbandry and prayers for a dry summer, or the plant can be left unclipped in the hope that air flow will lower its susceptibility. But if it's shaggy, then what's the point? Nothing takes as well as buxus to the blades of the shears. For that reason, it was the historic mainstay of English, French and Dutch formal gardens, the *sine qua non* of scribbled curlicues on the terrace and threaded knots of living green. For years we hunted an alternative hedging plant. 'Thinking outside the box' became a near-constant headline in the newspapers' gardening sections. Just as my colleagues concluded that in some places *only* box would do, even if it meant spraying, sweeping up each fallen leaf and ruthlessly cutting out any branch that shaded towards grey or brown, a second plague was sent down: caterpillars.

The box tree moth (*Cydalima perspectalis*) has attractive white wings with a mushroom-brown border. It is endemic to East Asia and can spread at six miles a year, meaning some sections of its journey to Camberwell were in the cargo hold of a boat, lorry or plane. In London it found abundant food and no predators. The population grew exponentially, reaching a peak in the long, hot summer of 2018. A rosebush being eaten by sawfly is beautiful next to the gorging of *Cydalima perspectalis*. Sawfly larvae hone down the leaf margin, their mouths on the edge of the blade, their little abdomens waving S-shaped in the air. Box tree moth caterpillars live in a sticky tunnel of soiled silk. They are ever-surrounded by excrement, shed skin and discarded head casings.

It is the digested matter, the frass, that is most upsetting to the horticulturalist, a trail of green pellets that passes through the mandible-tipped tube of organs as it hauls towards the next leaf. It is no doubt galling to see a topiary sphere costing as much as a second-hand car reduced to a stack of moth dung. But it teaches a valuable lesson: it was never your hedge, it was just a collection of stems and leaves, an attractive and well-plated lunch for diners who had not yet arrived.

When the caterpillars reached my workday garden, we picked them from between the stems and dropped them in a bucket of water. Birds would not touch them and, once drowned, they went into the compost heap. London's gardeners did less. In Dulwich I watched crisp, dwarf hedges succumb. At first they dented; someone might have been swinging at them with a hockey stick. The larvae were inside, gluing twigs into channels. Eating. It was slow at first, a smouldering creep, but inevitably they burst forth. Bushes were devoured. Some leaves were chewed to nothing, others were skeletonized, their browning remains trapped under the filthy web that spread over the bare stems and the giant, roaming larvae they harboured.

My daily cycle to Marylebone Station took me through Belgravia where things were worse. This was a land of off-shore billionaires' embassies, of four-storey stuccoed houses and private squares. Here, topiary was the acceptable decoration. Box cubes greeted dignitaries on the mission steps, there were pyramids on the first-floor balconies and little balls and cones in windowboxes. Black railings, white walls, green plants – the subtle uniform of power. The moths tore it all to pieces. Plants disintegrated on the ledges as if dosed with radiation. On Grosvenor Crescent, a street-long line of obelisks pitted and died like teeth in a bad dream.

The Regency terraces have not yet recovered their poise. Trailing ivy has been settled on for planters and clipped Delavay privet (*Ligustrum delavayanum*) is battling geometric yew (*Taxus baccata*) to become the expensively understated evergreen. Individually, the buildings will be more interesting, but I will miss cycling through on early May mornings with the dust and white-wine smell of box sharpening the air.

Belgravia is not the first place to lose its buxus. The plant is classed as a UK native and there is a scattered wild population. A grain of pollen was found in seven thousand-year-old subsoil from Sussex, proof of a long residence here. But I am inclined to believe that it only came in meaningful numbers with the Romans and that it largely left these shores when their culture fragmented. It was grown as an ornamental in the great villas of the Italian Peninsula. Pliny the Elder wrote of its use in decoration and named three distinct varieties (one of which was probably *Euonymus*). His nephew, Pliny the

Younger, described extensive boxwood planting around his own Tuscan home. Box hedges fronted the colonnade, hid dry stone walls and defined winding paths. Intricately patterned parterres divided plots of grass and fantastic animals in topiary work reared up on a bank. Excavations at Roman towns and villas give Britain its oldest preserved buxus leaves. They have been found at thirteen major towns, five ruined villas, four farmsteads and two religious sites, implying that the elite brought their familiar landscaping, along with their wine and oils, to this remote northern outpost. Buxus is also found in graves. A child buried at Scole in Norfolk some time in the 2nd century was interred with a wreath of box and nightshade. In Berkshire, a Romano-British woman was laid on a bed of box leaves and buried, while in Dorset archaeologists prized open a lead coffin to find the remains of an infant with a buxus crown about his head.

Box, the plant, was not named after box, the cuboid, as I once thought it was. It is an understandable mistake. A clipped box hedge is generally right-angled and as wide as it is tall. It is characteristically boxy. But the reverse is true. Boxes – cardboard, snuff, shoe, etc – are named after the little evergreen plant. The Ancient Greek word *puxís* gave us the Roman *buxus,* which was anglicized to 'box'. In the classical languages, it referred to the tree and the containers made from its wood, but words expand to fill gaps in the market. There was nothing sufficiently rectangular and lidded in the Saxon tongue and box got the job. It could instead have gone to the Ancient Greek *kóphinos*, meaning 'basket', and we'd put letters in a Royal Mail post coffin and play with windup Jack-in-the-coffins.

Not that any of the box plants that remained on Grove Park were particularly square. At No.6 there were the remains of one of the classic low hedges that guide a garden path to the front door. It had lived through horrible things and been cut back to ground level. The sliced ends of inch-thick stems poked through a furze of emerging leaves. I guessed moths forced the homeowner's hand, but it was the right thing to do. The old leaves and the eggs they harboured were gone and the new growth could get away before the next batch of mothers flew in. It is a good thing that shrubs cannot feel humiliation, because the plants were in danger of being overshadowed by the little herb roberts (*Geranium robertianum*) that once skulked in their shadows.

No.73 had the healthiest box on the Grove and shared it with 74 in the hedge that divided them. They were relaxed plants and their clipping had been loose and light. It gave them texture and probably saved them from blight. It seems to me that box tree moths must smell sap on the air like sharks smell blood in the water. At work we have tight box hedging around the terrace and it is perpetually infested. Down in the garden there is a blob that was once a sphere and is now growing out into a small tree, and an unmanaged hedge in the shade of some hornbeam. In recent years they have neither felt the shears nor had a single egg hatch upon them.

Back on Grove Park I found two box balls in square lead planters flanking the steps at No.16. Next door they sat as structural blobs in a smart, modern garden design. No.17 is a divided mansion. Once it was a place of respite and religious care, home to the nuns of our Lady of Cana. Their order sold it to Southwark Council who turned it into a children's home of the echoing, turreted kind that seems intuitively unfit for purpose. It fell into disuse in the 1980s and was squatted until the early 1990s when the council regained control and converted it into housing for homeless families. After a few decades it was again empty and the local authority sold it to a developer. Planning permission was granted to chop it into four and sell each slice as a smart terraced house. One of the attached conditions was that 'landscaped qualities' should soften the quartet of new front garden car parks, and that they should 'be of a high quality that would contribute positively'.

This explains the presence of the buxus. They are quint-essentially up-market and architectural. Their well-defined proportions allow the perennials around them to sprawl and mingle without any air of soft-stemmed dereliction.

These are some of the few gardens on the Grove that were borne from drawings in a studio. They excite me. Not the designs, which are all well done with nice plant choices, but their potential to fall apart. They were put in as clones, with identical shrubs, grasses and perennials, all from the same lorry and planted on the same day. But now they are under the care of separate freeholders and mutations will creep in. Each year they will grow more dissimilar as they warp to the hand that guides them. New owners will come and go, some will raze to the ground the work of their forebears, others might hide behind it, letting the chic blocks of yew grow out into tall churchyard trees. In thirty years' time they will be as unique and oddly put together as any other garden on the street and it will take a horticultural archaeologist to discover that once they were all alike.

City gardens change hands frequently. We inherit and we bequeath. It can be upsetting to see a loved space in the care of another. There is no use complaining, 'I drove past the other day and they've chopped down my acer.' It is a sad way to make conversation. Yes, they got rid of your plant, they also painted over your walls and put their fridge where yours once stood. Gardens have a life measured in centuries and will outgrow all their owners. As they say, 'Tis better to have loved and lost, than never to have loved at all.' The lines have worn thin from overuse, but they still hold true. The poem from which they are taken, Tennyson's *In Memoriam A H H*, examines life after the death of a precious friend. The stanza:

Till from the garden and the wild
A fresh association blow,
And year by year the landscape grow
Familiar to the stranger's child

should be read with hope. Life continues, even after that which was most beautiful has left it. Arthur Henry Hallam might have gone, but other brilliant boys would meet at Cambridge, even while Tennyson grew old and skated alone on his pond, scarf flapping behind him in the dark. We will all be forgotten, and so will the gardens we created. We might live for a bit in the memories of those that knew us, or in the overgrown relics of our planting plans, but only as ghosts. Not long from now, box will leave Camberwell. It will linger in heritage horticulture, but the days when it was *the* plant of domestic design are over. Never again will Tom Stuart-Smith stun the gardening world by pairing it with white astrantia and Baltic parsley for the Laurent-Perrier garden at Chelsea. In thirty years' time, Stuart-Smith will be retired, Laurent-Perrier will be sponsoring techno for old timers, and some plant that we've all ignored will be the epitome of cool. But the fact that it won't happen again does not make Tom's garden any less beautiful, nor London's box years any less significant. I am glad to have lived through them and to be given the chance to see what will grow in their place.

# 8

## APPLE

On the last day of August, baby Solomon was stung by a wasp. His incomprehension was heart-breaking. Until that moment, pain had always been the result of something definite, but he did not see the insect creep under his never-walked-upon foot. And even if he had, how could it be the cause of this? A hurt as big as falling head first on the kitchen floor or shutting his fingers in the desk yet another time.

Could it happen again, his teary eyes asked. I'm afraid it could, it probably will. That venomous spike has punctured your innocence, as well as your skin, I should have said. Instead I hugged him and wibbled my bottom lip with a forefinger. The funny noise did not work its magic. Summer had ended. It was time to stack our glasses, leave the pub garden and head for home.

We walked back under horse chestnuts already crisp and shedding leaves. We had entered autumn – the season of the wasp.

That striped criminal had been lured by a glass of cold cider; rather fitting, as apples are the fruit of lost innocence and cider its drink. When I was a schoolboy I was brought back home in a near cider-coma by a policeman. I remember a blurry yellow jacket and black trousers talking to my mother in her dressing gown. I'm told I was polite in a slurred way, saying things like: 'Mumble, mumble, mumble, officer', which were taken as apologies. For Eve, another sinner tempted by the apple, forgiveness has been harder to find.

Down the road from Grove Park there are Eve's children. On Camberwell Green, cider is taken from soon after it gets light until well after dark, mostly from black cans marked with a red 'K'. To the east, where Choumert Road meets Bellenden, it is the same, though the atmosphere down there is less frenetic; there are fewer sirens and no street preachers. In December, a Christmas tree was put up in front of the horseshoe of benches and it looked festive and sad as, of course, the season should. Despite its proximity and pleasantness, none of the drinkers ever uses the Grove. There are no corner shops, the air is residential and there is not enough of the world passing by. There are apples of a sort though.

Five degrees north of the equator, across the Atlantic Ocean, lies Villa de Leyva, a colonial town in the high semi-desert of the Colombian Andes. In the thin air between the fossilized kronosaurus and the bright blue sulphuric pools there are orchards. In 2016 I drove up from Bogotá for a weekend and witnessed their artificial winter. Apples need a period of dormancy, a complete reset, enough to shunt them out of growth and into flower production. In Eurasia this is granted by plummeting temperatures and the resultant leaf drop. Villa de Leyva relies on a *campesino* in a plaid shirt stripping the branches with brutal, eel-skinning jerks. With the apical buds gone, the plant is free to limp into an approximation of spring and the blossom it brings.

The apples were there because we were there. They are domesticated trees. They follow humans like dogs and goats. In 1862, Henry David Thoreau noted in *The Atlantic* that 'Blossom-Week, like the Sabbath, is thus annually spreading over the prairies; for when man migrates, he carries with him not only his birds, quadrupeds, insects, vegetables, and his very sword, but his orchard also.' When the great transcendentalist of Walden Pond saw the European, his religion and his trees drawing ever-closer to the Pacific, he saw the future: apple orchards now cover over fourteen thousand acres of California.

Almost all the apples produced in the Golden State are Gala, Fuji, Granny Smith or Pink Lady; sweet eaters, all of them, as shiny and blemish-free as the joggers on Laguna Beach.

Not that the British varieties are any more natural. We have turned them into monstrous over-croppers. I have spent time in abandoned orchards (care of the 2017 cider crash – they thought we'd be drinking it on ice forever, but the rise of rosé put paid to that). Limbs hung from the trees, their twigs lost in the ascending furze of bracken and bramble. Some were decorated with still-reddening apples between bunches of withered leaves, others held last year's mummified fruit. They had all been torn down by the weight of the unpicked harvest.

Robert Hogg's *The British Pomology*, published in 1851, is a salute to the apple breeders, ancient and modern, who got us to the state where 'a good year' means trees splintering beneath their own bounty. The book gives us names and flavours to conjure with: Toker's Incomparable ('yellowish, firm, crisp, tender, juicy, and marrow-like, with a brisk and pleasant acid'), Hoary Morning ('marked with broad pale stripes on the shaded side'), Red Streaked Rawling ('abounding in a sweet and pleasant juice'), Harvey's Wiltshire Defiance ('very handsome and most desirable') and Herefordshire Monster ('a small cider apple'). These and hundreds more were selected from the now-forgotten seedlings that rose in orchards, nurseries, hedgerows and gardens. Some were chance discoveries, others deliberate attempts to breed in traits. But they all have a ten-thousand-year ancestry stretching back to when man first started to cultivate and harvest their wild relatives in the mountains of Kazakhstan.

Of course, ten thousand years is nothing to an evolutionary biologist. They would point out that apples were manipulating humans before humans were even human. They are bribes for mammals, nothing more. A payment in return for the promise of seed dispersal. The first grape-sized things we might recognize as apples appeared around nine million years ago in the late Miocene era. They would have been eaten by ground-feeding mammals such as the prehistoric rhinoceros *Brachypotherium brachypus*, a so-called 'dirty browser', whose fossilized teeth show that it frequently consumed food straight from the gritty earth. We're not so different from extinct rhinos, you and I, not in the evolutionary scale that stretches from amoeba to zebra. We share much of our genetic material with the extinct mega fauna, genes such as TAS1R1, which code for sugar-receptive proteins in the excitable cells of our mouths. These are found in white mice, blue whales and everything in between. Mammal tongues are literally electrified by apple flesh and the pleasure we derive from it is hardwired. A brain that loves ripe fruit is a brain attached to a body that survives the winter.

Unripe apples taste horrid. And rightly so. The tree derives no benefit from having a hippopotamodon eat from its branches before the seeds have developed. Sugar floods the fruit only at the last moment. They are designed to be sucked down almost rotten, but not quite. Once the fruit has actively begun to rot, the seeds lose viability and animals are warned away by the rise in a highly toxic molecule called ethanol. Fortunately, or perhaps not, around ten million years ago, a gibbon-like ancestor of the great apes suffered a mutation on chromosome 4 (gene ADH4), which greatly improved the function of a single dehydrogenase enzyme and allowed alcohol to form a component of its diet – in Camberwell we are still living with the consequences.

Dr Lettsom of Grove Hill was a Quaker. Along with other members of the Society of Friends, he extolled abstinence and clean living, and as a practising physician he was familiar with overconsumption. His pamphlet of 1789, *History of Some of the Effects of Hard Drinking,* is as concise and clear-eyed a description of chronic alcoholism as found in any contemporary textbook. The nurses and doctors over at Kings College Hospital, two streets from where his house once stood, would surely be able to match the symptoms he describes to their modern clinical labels: belly pain increasing to such excess that the miserable sufferer is obliged to press against a table (acute pancreatitis); breath that smells like rotten apples (alcoholic ketoacidosis); legs as smooth as polished ivory and the soles of the feet glassy and shining (alcoholic oedema).

But Grove Park in the late eighteenth century was not a place of complete sobriety and temperance. Lettsom was a friend of James Boswell, the lawyer who authored *The Life of Samuel Johnson*. According to one historian, Boswell was also the first alcoholic of public record. This was a man who got drunk and kissed strangers at funerals, who stubbornly downed bottles of claret under the disapproving glare of his sober peers then ran off in search of prostitutes, who was inebriated at his father's deathbed, smashed windows in pubs that refused to serve him, threw chairs at his wife, and wrote again and again about waking up miserably humbled and ashamed.

Some of the drinking took place on ground I now walk in search of these front garden stories. On the slope where number No.90 Grove Park stands, Lettsom had his Temple of Sybil, a rotunda filled with curios from the South Seas, with an elevated deck for viewing the glory of the cosmos by night and Peckham by day. Boswell was a frequent visitor and boasts of reciting his

*Horatian Ode to Charles Dilly* in the temple. One of the verses of that poem contains the excruciating rhyme:

> Methinks you laugh to hear but half
> The name of Dr Lettsom
> From him of good- talk, liquors food,-
> His guests will always get some.

Lettsom himself penned a gently admonishing letter to Boswell in the aftermath of one of his visits to Camberwell. The doctor tactfully notes that he has recently been able to view his friend in some 'interesting situations', where 'thy whole soul has been poured out in social enjoyment', before warning that 'such conviviality' would likely kill him, something no man of refinement would wish for. It was probably the doctor's Tortuga punch that did for Boswell in the rotunda, but were he around today, it might well have been strong cider.

Lettsom planted two hundred and seventeen apple trees at Grove Hill, including eight Franklin's Golden Pippins ('vigorous, healthy, and hardy'), six Golden Russets ('firm, crisp, sugary, and aromatic; but not abounding in juice') and three specimens of an apple he calls Arrow's Incomparable. He also had an arbustum, or orchard, with two hundred generic apple trees. That orchard now lies directly beneath the tarmac and houses of Grove Park. On old estate plans, it is labelled 'K'. Each year the crop was sold and it is likely some of it went into cider production, which rather beautifully means that Camberwell was once a producer of 'K' cider, as well as its consumer.

Lettsom's trees stood for at least twenty years after he was forced to sell his estate, surviving the tenures of William Whitten, solicitor, and Charles Baldwin, newspaper man. In 1836 they were listed as 'fruit garden' and auctioned to Mr Chadwick, a railway magnate, at Garraway's Coffee House. Could they be living still? Might they somehow have survived the coming of the trains, the cutting of Grove Park, the Victorian builders, the smog, war-time allotmenteers, 1970s droughts and 1990s decking? No, of course not. They would now be the same age as the oldest-known *Malus domestica*, the original Bramley planted by Mary Ann Brailsford at the beginning of the nineteenth century, a tree under the constant gaze of the world's greatest pomologists and still inexorably dying. Lettsom's russets and pippins were planted in an eccentric Eden on the edge of a ravenous and ever-expanding city. They never stood a chance.

So why have I spent so much time looking for them? In September I walked slowly up and down the street, hovering in the gaps between houses, hoping to glimpse an impossibly ancient stump with perhaps a few scab-blackened fruits clinging to its remaining branches. In December, Sol and I rode the train from East Dulwich to Peckham Rye, and Peckham Rye to Denmark Hill, tracing two sides of a fat-yet-sharp triangle like a finch's beak. I was looking for unexpected flares of green in the bare twigs, apples often keeping their leaves through to Christmas when the other trees have given up and gone to bed. There were none, the orchard was gone. There were, however, other members of the genus *Malus* to provide us with glorious consolation.

Dr Johnson, another of Lettsom's friends, claimed to have known a clergyman's family brought up on apple dumplings, but man needs more than fruit to survive. Grove Park is no longer productive and its apples are ornamental, but they are more important for that. In this part of London, apples are easy to find: the Sainsbury's on Dog Kennel Hill has them from Argentina, Chile, France, Italy and Spain. Cider is even more readily available; there are twelve off-licences around Camberwell Green alone. What this city suburb needs is beauty. The crab apples of Grove Park are a rebuke to traffic lights and traffic, to chicken bones in the gutter and large cars on small pavements. They are pretty things in a world trending towards ugliness, a year-round solace and seduction to the walker in no particular hurry.

A warm morning in late April is best for wasting time with crab apples. Their blossom is the quintessence of the season, on a twig-for-twig basis more spring-like than any flowering cherry's. The five-petalled blooms tend to bud pink and break white, opening at the same time as the young leaves, each as soft and perfect as a baby's foot. After a winter spent kicking grey stones over greasy pavements, they make one want to turn into a tree-eating herbivore, to wrap a long tongue round the branch and suck down all the promise of T-shirts and summer tans. It's partially a scent hunger; they smell like roses without the musk, but with a note of citrus where the sweetness ought to be. On Grove Park, the 'Red Sentinel' has a better perfume than the 'Golden Hornet' but both are worth adding five minutes to any journey for.

The second great season for crab apples is winter. My mother has a 'Red Sentinel' on an extremely dwarfing rootstock in her small garden. It is at its best in December when its berry-like fruit hang in pyracantha clusters, and at its most valuable in late January when all other colour has fallen from the garden and Christmas is just a memory on the bathroom scales. My sister once hosted an over-attended birthday party, with teenage hooligans running riot and passing out in the toilet. The house was put back together the next day, but no one could reattach the crab apple's fruit. Some boys had pulled them all off to throw at each other. To deprive a keen gardener of her winter solace and make her think of the senselessness of man every time she stood at the window to do the washing-up was a sinful act indeed.

Grove Park's other crab apple is 'Golden Hornet', a yellow-fruiting variety with dark pink buds. It does not allow its fruit to drop, letting each one shrivel on the bough and rot next to its melon-yellow neighbours. Squinted at, these withering formations do actually look like a nest of hornets – a mass of red-brown thoraxes, golden heads and black-striped abdomens – though it's hard to imagine that John Waterer, who introduced it to the market in 1948, named it for its resemblance to a mass of seething insects.

Men like John should be thanked for their services in breeding beauty onto our streets. The wild crab apples are lovely things, and to find them blossoming low and sparse, or fruiting in a country hedgerow, is a treat. But Camberwell is an artificial place of exaggerated problems; we need trees bred for their exaggerated beauty and artificial solutions. That we have these cultivars, not just of crab apple but magnolia, peonies, camellias and roses, is testament to a fundamental human desire to make our surroundings slightly more attractive. Centuries of effort, much of it by amateurs, has gone into producing pretty flowers and long-hanging fruit, for the benefit of the eye and not the belly. The presence of the 'Red Sentinel' and the 'Golden Hornet' on Grove Park shows us that despite the apple-driven sins of Eve, and of me, of teenage boys and all cider drinkers, man is still full up with goodness.

Before this land was Lettsom's it was walked by the young William Blake. On Peckham Rye, angels revealed themselves to him, bespangling a tree's boughs like stars, and he mourned for the lost loveliness of the Camberwell hills in *Jerusalem*. His poem *A Poison Tree* compares a long grudge to a tree:

And I waterd it in fears,
Night & morning with my tears:
And I sunned it with smiles,
And with soft deceitful wiles.

And it grew both day and night.
Till it bore an apple bright.
And my foe beheld it shine,
And he knew that it was mine.

And into my garden stole,
When the night had veild the pole;
In the morning glad I see;
My foe outstretched beneath the tree.

It is a stark and strictly allegorical warning. But humans water their trees with hopes, not fears. For ten thousand years we have been nurturing apples without malice but with love; love for our family and friends, hoping to make our situation and theirs better, sweeter, tastier. Our hope for better was strong enough to breed a whole new species, *Malus domestica*, then splinter it into a thousand parts. And we are not done yet; there will be more apples in the future, even more adaptable and juicy. They are growing them now in Villa de Leyva, in Nigeria, Tasmania and Uganda. The world might heat up, go to war and flood itself, but as long as there are humans in Camberwell, there will be apples growing here and all might not be lost.

# 9

## *VERBENA BONARIENSIS*

In the summer before Solomon was born, I spent my Wednesday evenings in the London Metropolitan Archives. Dusty and hot from a day in the garden, I'd ride the train back to Marylebone then cycle to Clerkenwell and the climate-controlled cool of the LMA, emerging two hours later with the night still warm and friends nearby for a pint. Generally, I was looking at records related to Victorian public landscapes, and though I'm sure they were interesting, I have forgotten most of what I read. One document, however, stays with me.

At the top of the yellowing page was a small notice: 'Private – For Members of Parks Committee only'. Below, a brief note stated that an inquiry had been called to investigate the 'doings at Finsbury Park'. Reading on, I found the story of

Mr Cochrane, who had appeared twenty years earlier to oversee some labourers and never left. At some point he slipped free from the bureaucrats at the Metropolitan Board of Works, consolidated power and turned vigilante, building his own Heart of Darkness between the bandstand and the boating lake. He was only discovered in 1889 when the Board of Works was abolished and replaced by the London County Council. The paper I held was Cochrane's personal testimony:

Question: Since Mr McKenzie left, who has supervised you?
Cochrane: No one.

Question: Although you have been alluded to as Park Superintendent, there is, I believe, no actual minute so appointing you?
Cochrane: There is not.

Question: Is it true that you have ever thrashed with a stick, whilst other men held them, persons who have committed offences against the Bye-laws?
Cochrane: I have done so when there has been no evidence on which a magistrate would convict, but I thought them guilty and punished them.

Question: Did you once tar the private parts of one such man?
Cochrane: Yes; an organ grinder. An old man. They were
tarring the paths at the time.

Further examination reveals another offender having his nose
near-severed and losing the sight in one eye, and that Cochrane
kept a cow in the park and profited from its milk, had employees
look after his chickens, sold municipal plants to private citizens,
tampered with evidence relating to the attempted assassination
of Queen Victoria in the 'Jubilee Plot' and hid gardeners in the
rockeries as spies.

It is a pity Cochrane turned his talents to violence. He
evidently had the characteristics Christopher Lloyd thought
important for someone in charge of a public landscape.
Concluding a scathing review of Wisley, the Royal
Horticultural Society's flagship garden, Lloyd wrote: 'One
cannot expect inspiration from an institutional garden, unless
it is under the command of an exceptionally strong-willed
gardener, who can overcome public opinion from below and
committee direction from above.'

Lloyd was particularly disappointed by the long borders
down at Wisley and the way they were planted according to
height, with the smallest flowers at the front and the largest

at the back. He called it both sensible and predictable, and urged his readers to break the rules and bring tall specimens to the flower bed's edge. For this he suggested stemmy, thin-textured plants like angel's fishing rod (*Dierama pulcherrimum*) and wafty grasses like golden oats (*Stipa gigantea*). Best of all would be *Verbena bonariensis*.

How I agree. *Verbena bonariensis* is a plant to be looked through. It has grown in England since arriving from Buenos Aires in 1726 but in the past few decades it has risen to a prominence that borders on ubiquity. Near the front of a height-graded border it is a five-foot cloud of semi-transparent purple with all the obstructive power of a flight of butterflies. In front gardens it should be set as close to the road as possible, so that anyone looking in does so through a jewelled veil. In Grove Park in mid-September I found it flowering happily after a long summer in a south-facing garden. No.125, possessor of the verbena, is the first house a walker encounters after leaving Camberwell Grove and is something of a bridge between the late-Victorian semis of Grove Park and the Georgian terraces of its illustrious neighbour. It was built around 1845, but its style is firmly Regency. White stucco covers the brickwork and a stone balustrade does the work of a garden wall. The building has a bold cornice and a parapet that partially obscures the blue slate roof. Once it would have been home to a single family and their servants. Now it contains flats A to E.

Which makes *Verbena bonariensis* an excellent choice for the garden. It is a flower about which no one could argue. It looks good in gravel gardens, where it stands straight and surprisingly strong, with no need for softer plants to hide its legs, and is equally at home in lush tropical borders – I grow it as a purple haze over dahlias and cannas. It can be formal, filling the narrow beds of a modern parterre, or wild, planted in a perennial meadow with grasses below. The colour goes with everything. It is salt in horticulture's cuisine, an enhancer of flavours. The rigidity of its stems makes an underplanting of Mexican feathergrass (*Nassella tenuissima*) all the more wispy, and the almost-metallic brightness of its tiny flowers brings out the soft, dew-dipped nature of a pink floribunda rose. No matter what the disparate residents of No.125 Grove Park think a garden should be, they must all agree it should contain *Verbena bonariensis*. How could they not?

Strong personalities and clashing tastes meet in the garden at which I work. *Verbena bonariensis* is our glue – the plant we all agree on. And we need these pieces of common ground. There is generally tension between a head gardener and the employer and we are not exempt. My clients see the Cochrane in me.

A desire to take over and make the landscape my own. Worse still, they can tell I disagree with some of the jobs I'm given, and no one likes paying to be resented in their own garden. In my defence, I need these proprietorial feelings to do my best work, and I couldn't possibly stay if I felt I was not contributing to the world's beauty. To be a full-time gardener is to sign on for a lifetime of low wages in the service of giving someone richer than you a better view. I don't own any of the land I work but I *do* own some of the beauty, and when I'm asked to damage it I feel real pain.

Arthur Clutton-Brock understood the clash between employer and gardener and wrote on it a century ago in his classic book *Studies in Gardening*:

> The consequence of this conflict in tastes may be some real unhappiness to the gardener. He has his duty to his employer of course, and he can only keep his place by doing it. But he also has his artistic conscience.

Clutton-Brock writes from the garden-owner's perspective, naturally. He was a horticulturally enlightened man of his times, riding the wave of 'Wild Gardening' and joyfully undoing the work of all those stuffy Victorians. He saw head gardeners as dated traditionalists, still wedded to the old system where their control of the hot-house thermostat placed them in a position of power. 'The amateur in gardening is revolutionary, the professional a conservative,' he wrote. Nowadays this has reversed. Head gardeners are no longer proud men with walrus moustaches. They are passionate creatives and quite likely to be women. It is now the paid gardener who champions wildness and fights for haze, waft and scruff; for softened plantings that evoke moods beyond simply 'neat' or 'colourful'. Their clients, meanwhile, yearn for something bright and cheerful that doesn't flop over every time it rains. To both parties I say, '*Verbena bonariensis*'.

To return to Christopher Lloyd and his attack on Wisley, his words appeared in *Country Life* over thirty years ago. Lloyd has since died and his own garden, Great Dixter, has become an institution itself. Remarkably, it remains the most inspirational space in UK horticulture. That it has not become a museum to 'Christo' but continues to innovate and improve is down, in part, to its own strong-willed head gardener (and now chief executive), Fergus Garrett. But it is more than that. Every gardener who works there, every volunteer, seems to have fallen under the spell of the place. They are acolytes, part of a blissed-out, rural beauty cult, doing the best work of their careers in the service of a higher cause. Metre by metre Great Dixter is the best garden in England because, metre by metre, it is the garden most worshipped by its attendants.

I'm sure this is because the staff don't have to wear uniforms. How is one supposed to think creatively in a polo shirt and matching fleece? More importantly, how is one supposed to recruit people who care deeply about aesthetics when you have a glorified PE kit waiting for them to change into? I have worked in uniformed gardening jobs (one in ambulance-driver green, the other in navy blue) and 'wear what you like' jobs. I design better borders in my own jumper and jacket than I do in a branded anorak.

My first encounter with *Verbena bonariensis* came in one of these uniformed jobs. On the day I took up my role as a very junior horticulturalist, the expressionless Head of Security handed me two pairs of green trousers, five green shirts, two green fleece jackets and a pair of black boots, then sent me off to join the other gardeners. Thus decked out we looked so obviously part of the grounds team that we became anonymous. For the chefs, house girls, cleaners and drivers we were 'the gardeners', unless we were on our own when we were 'one of the gardeners'. Likewise, they were known to us by their aprons, hats and pinafores. 'Who's putting cigarette butts in the flower pots?' we might ask. 'I don't know, ask the drivers.' 'Who emptied bleach on the hedge?' 'No idea, maybe the cleaners?'

The expectation was that we look neat and orderly and keep the garden the exact same way. We were addressed interchangeably, worked weekends interchangeably and gardened interchangeably. We even began to regard each other as interchangeable, until one of my colleagues designed the most magnificent rose garden. It was just roses, cider gum (*Eucalyptus gunnii*) and *Verbena bonariensis*. The eucalyptus was cut down on rotation, so its stems were always fresh and blue, and the roses were repeat flowerers in dusky pink. Together they were striking but it was the verbena that impressed me. It was utterly out of control, anarchic and waving about, mingling with itself and the rose sprays and yet somehow not attracting the ire of the property managers. Until then I had been gardening with my head down, trying to fill space and keep things tidy; that verbena showed me that, no matter how hard the brief, as long as there was space to plant, there was room to feed the soul.

This is not to say all gardens should be art, they are too practical for that, particularly small domestic gardens where paths are placed because they lead to the shed. They might curve and snake, flirt with tickling grasses and duck beneath the hanging boughs, but ultimately their destination is always the lawnmower, hardly a transcendental goal. The essayist Walter Pater wrote that, 'All art constantly aspires to the condition of music.' But it is impossible for a garden to marry form and content as perfectly as a symphony when it must contain the washing line and a bird feeder.

There have been exceptions. Derek Jarman's garden at Dungeness was as close to 'garden as pure garden' as it gets. But not all of us want to have a borderless expanse of flotsam and poppy; we want somewhere to drink wine with our friends and lovers, and we want a big fence so the neighbours don't watch us doing it. We want a useable garden with floral decorations – this is what every garden designer is selling.

It is more obvious in urban gardens than their rural counterparts, which have room to hide their utilitarian nature. In London we make do with half a tennis court each, on average. That's one service box for the shed, another for the grass, the back box for outdoor tables, chairs, barbecues and the like, with just the tramlines left over for any flowers, shrubs, apple trees and ivy. Things are worse if there are children in the house. Then there is the plastic slide and a paddling pool to fit in. As the writer and critic Cyril Connolly might have said, there is no more sombre enemy of good art than the trampoline on the lawn.

All this must make front gardens the space of art, if there can be any such space. Aside from storing bins and getting us to the door, most front gardens have no practical use. We are not a nation that sits on the threshold watching the cars and nodding to the world. Human time in these places is limited to the minutes we actually spend gardening; for the rest of the month they belong to the plants and the passersby. This makes them somehow less selfish and more universal. At No.125 Grove Park the *Verbena bonariensis* flowered from the end of June until the middle of October. Seventeen weeks of beauty, all of it pointless and wonderful and shared with the wanderers on the road.

Enjoying verbena connects me to the residents of 125, though I have never met them. It also keeps me close to my employers who, despite our differences of opinion about growing clematis into the trees, letting *Geranium maderense* spread through the tropical garden, and keeping elderflowers too pruned to flower, are wonderful people. They give me an inordinate amount of creative and budgetary freedom and are exceptionally good fun, but still, there is that slight dissonance. In *The New Gardening* of 1913, Walter P Wright astutely recognized that an estate owner's relationship with the head gardener is necessarily different from that with his other members of staff:

> The old labourer in the village, the old shepherd, the old groom, may become the pet of the family, the old gardener never...he is too used to resenting the intrusions of his employers to ever idolise them in the way the other servants might.

Thankfully, this is not always true. One of my favourite gardener and client relationships, that between the society photographer Cecil Beaton and his man at Reddish House, Jack Smallpiece, is seen only obliquely in the pages of Beaton's diary. Entries are often mean-spirited and excoriating. Katharine Hepburn is a dried-up boot, a rotten ingrained viper, it is incredible that she can be exhibited in public. Marlene Dietrich is a liar, an egomaniac and a bore. However, when Beaton writes of his garden, and particularly his gardener, a softer, happier man shines through. Smallpiece is portrayed as a bent and ancient figure, peering in terror from his cottage window when fireworks are set off, but who becomes fifteen years younger, 'his years of fatigue forgotten', when visitors praise his flowers.

Beaton's commentary often comes across as the affectionate witterings of a Bright Young Thing – down from London for the weekend and enjoying watching the work of a picturesque and venerable old rustic. But I have seen Smallpiece – he appears for few seconds in the background of David Bailey's 1971 documentary, *Beaton by Bailey*. Cecil Beaton and Jack Smallpiece are identical in age and appearance, two thin, grey-haired pensioners in tweed jackets, tottering around together in the garden. The only thing to tell them apart is that one carries a spade and the other wears a giant silk cravat. Beaton's last-ever diary entry, a week before he died, is about the loss of his cat, Timothy. He breaks down in tears and writes, 'Timmy had been a great friend of Smallpiece and me.' Reading this entry, one realizes that in his later years Cecil's real life did not happen when he was in New York, Paris or Monte Carlo, but when he was sitting on the sunny side of the lane and squabbling with his gardener over the affections of a cat.

Walter P Wright advised employers to show tolerance towards their head gardener as, 'his virtues are real, even if they are obscured by exasperating foibles'. Is it any wonder the senior horticulturalist becomes a boorish tyrant, he muses. After all, 'he has plunged straight from school into an absorbing and overmastering profession, which has filled his untrained mind to overflowing'. Look beyond this and try to see his faults as virtues: 'A man obsessed with a great love for plants has an innate nobility of character which should secure him respect, and it is lamentable that surface faults should be allowed to obscure his real worth.'

My surface fault is wanting more disarray in a garden that needs to be pristine – ready at any time for croquet and champagne. *Verbena bonariensis* allows me some chaos, seeding where it likes and meshing groups of plants together. Luckily it is spectacular enough never to be mistaken for a weed. I am content because there is some shift and movement in the borders, things to tell one summer from another. My employers are satisfied because they still have a high-maintenance garden with lots of 'wow factor'. No one needs to wear a polo shirt, be held down, thrashed or tarred – verbena allows us to muddle along contentedly. It lies, with tulips in the long grass, in that happy place where our separate lines of beauty cross and for a moment twine together.

# LONDON PLANE

In the mid-1830s a well was sunk in Grove Lane. When interviewed, the foreman of the diggers described sixty feet of gravel, clay and sand, followed by a six-inch layer of dark, friable, earthy matter, then clay alone for thirty feet before clear water began to pool. In the earthy matter he found a large lump of peacock coal, and showed it to local geologist and antiquarian Douglas Allport, who pronounced it a fine specimen.

Peacock coal is pure anthracite, the prince of coals. It is black with an oil-on-water iridescence. The discovery raises the prospect of a seam of perfect coal below Camberwell and an alternative history for Southeast London, one where the bankers of Dulwich commute to work past sooty men up from a night in the mines. It is not so impossible – in the 1940s there were productive coal works down the A2 at Cobham in Surrey.

John Burroughs, the American conservationist, believed that a man takes root at his feet and that 'he is no more than a potted plant in his house or carriage, till he has established communication with the soil by the loving and magnetic touch of his soles to it'. We Londoners are potted plants, for sure. There is no connection between our shoes and the soil. One only has to look at my hallway to know that. There are three flats in our building, with six people between them. Discounting the baby, that's ten trips to work and ten returns a day. A lot of traffic passes over the woollen carpet and yet it remains dove-grey.

London might sit on clay, but it's so capped by roads and buildings that the underlying geology seems of purely academic interest. That is, until it dries out in a heatwave and the walls start cracking. It is all still there. Those vanished fields are only a foot away. Roads are nothing. Compared to the earth, they are oil on the ocean. It only costs a couple of thousand pounds to hire a caterpillar-tracked asphalt mill for a night and a day. With fifty pounds from each of my neighbours, I could grind out our entire road on a Thursday and have the start of an orchard planted by the end of the weekend.

In July 2019, eighty delegates met in City Hall, Norman Foster's glass bladder snail by the Thames, for the first London Plane Tree Conference. Professor Chris Baines shared his theory that plane trees survive in London because of leaks in the water mains. The inefficient, ever-rotting veins of the capital form a city-wide irrigation system, a giant alkathene, gaffer tape, iron and plastic version of the drip hose I wind under newly planted hedges. Certainly I have never seen a plane tree die through drought, though in hot weather they shed their bark.

Grove Park is a plane tree street. There are sixty-one of them, each of them taller than the houses. They are stronger than any road surface and heave up the pavements. Here is our visible connection with the earth below. Each is a link between the sky and soil, the light of the sun and the wet of the ground. There surely is nothing closer to alchemy than the transmutation of a colourless gas ($CO_2$) and a transparent liquid (water) into a hundred and twenty feet of trunk and olive-green branch with enough potential energy to come through the roof and kill a man while he brushes his teeth.

We are lucky that plane trees rarely fall over. In October I found myself awake through an overnight storm. A virus had stuck in Solomon's chest, leaving him panicked and struggling to breathe. He eventually found some sleep, upright on my lap, and I sat through the small hours while the wind built outside. It sounded apocalyptic, each gust shredding on the big sycamore and reforming to shake our windows in their frames. The pitch came at 5am. Bins boomed as they overturned and I held the boy tight as all around vegetation thrashed in the darkness.

From my chair it seemed impossible that anything growing could survive. The maples would be snapped and the wall roses pulped on the bricks that supported them. Dawn came late. I took Sol in to his mother and sat with a cup of tea, waiting for the damage to be revealed. The light brought a scene of shocking normality. The salvias were in flower and the dahlias still held their petals. The apple was upright and the big sycamore waved a crown of yellow leaves. I went up to the bedroom and found Solomon playing happily on the duvet, smiling and shouting, pink-cheeked with oxygen and joy.

Gardening has prepared me for the worries of parenthood: I've had years of jolting awake, convinced I've killed something precious; that I've left the greenhouse open or sprayed herbicide in place of fertilizer. In the morning everything is usually fine, but still, I walked up to Grove Park to see if the gardens had survived. In *Ghost Trees*, his treatise on nature in the fissures of East London, Bob Gilbert muses on planes and 'that strange propensity of a tree to be young and old at the same time and in the same body'. The Giants of the Grove were planted in 1895, when men still wore frock coats and upright collars. They are older now and swollen, with gnarls and galls and huge bulges like the nests of tropical bees. Yet up beyond their fattened ankles, the planes are throwing out stems as fresh as in their second summer, the year when the requirement for motorcars to be preceded by a flag-bearer was dropped and London began its regrettable descent into driving.

The London plane copes better with air pollution than humans, who are suffocated every year in their thousands by neighbours choosing to pop to the shops and drop off their children in an SUV. The tree's success may lie in its vaunted ability to shed bark and thus clear the gas-exchange structures known as lenticels. In the nineteenth century, their flaking skin was a useful demonstration of how filthy the city, and everything in it, was. A piece would slough off and reveal a brooch of grey-green, incongruous against the stained wood.

How beautiful and horrible this reminder of nature under the grime must have been to the Victorians. Two years before our trees were planted, *The Spectator* ran a lyrical and impassioned defence of growing trees in London's fouled air. It argued that most things would live through the smoke. The author had seen mulberry trees in gloomy city gardens. He knew copper beeches, thorns of many kinds and an urban copse of weeping birch. Yes, he was able to rub white paper on a cedar by the Albert Gate and find it black in his hand, but this was not the reason cedars no longer grew in Hammersmith and West Kensington. For that, he suggested, we should blame greed and the builder's trowel. One paragraph even made a poetic argument for grime increasing the beauty of a plant: day-old spring leaves look all the more fresh and perfect in front of coal-black boughs. Most observers would not agree. I am reminded of the French critic Hippolyte Taine's report on the capital in 1885:

It seems as if the livid and sooty fog had even befouled the verdure of the parks. But what most offends the eyes are the colonnades, peristyles, Grecian ornaments, mouldings and wreathes of the houses, all bathed in soot; poor antique architecture – what is it doing in such a climate?

The best planes I know are the Oriental planes (*Platanus orientalis*) that grow on Crete. These are the trees that shaded Zeus and Europa as they begot King Minos. Under that fierce sun, their desert camo makes sense. In London, planes seem too dry, too coated in hair, too keen to catch at the back of the throat. What are they *doing* in such a climate? I suppose the only answer is surviving. We don't know how long for, not because they are threatened by disease (although they are), but because they are such a new creation that we have no idea of their natural life span.

The tree is a hybrid, born of lovers that evolved with the Atlantic between them. Its parents are Zeus's *Platanus orientalis,* from Asia and the Eastern Mediterranean, and the American Sycamore, *Platanus occidentalis.* The cross-pollination happened some time in the seventeenth century, probably in Spain. A plane growing at the Château de Chessy in the Rhône was reportedly planted in the 1620s and there are trees from the 1660s in Saxony and Cambridgeshire. London's oldest is at Barn Elms and has probably sat there since the 1680s. As yet we have no idea when the cells and sapwood of these trees will give up. They may find their limit at six hundred years or they might live another two millennia.

After the storm I found that the sixty-one Giants of Grove Park all remained, still in the race to be the world's first two-thousand-year-old London plane. It was blowy when I reached them. A pigeon shot over the houses, fast as a falcon on the wind from Dulwich. It skidded past the tree by No.26, hanging for a moment in the gale before beating back into the canopy. The branches shook stiffly, all of them ten feet long and growing from three-year-old pollarding cuts. The limbs from which they sprouted barely moved at all. Trees as sturdy as these can seem impervious to the blows of man and weather. So it is a shock to see a large one felled. Something that had been a landmark for generations suddenly disappears, leaving a gap that feels four times as big as the tree ever was. It seems wrong that something so monumental can just go, as if a hill had moved off over the course of a morning. It's worse when one looks at the tree surgeons, usually three blokes, sitting on fresh logs and eating their foil-wrapped sandwiches by a pile of brushwood and sawdust. It doesn't seem right that so much change can be wrought so casually and before lunchtime.

On Saturday the 19th of April 1910, *The Gardener's Magazine* reported 'Vandalism at Camberwell' at how some of the one hundred and twenty plane trees on Grove Park had been mistreated. A gang of workers from the Borough Council had descended and hacked at them until they 'resembled a line of washing line poles'. According to sources, our trees had then been fifteen years old and flourishing.

We can thank or blame those workmen for the look of the Grove's trees today: bare and branchless to a height of six metres. Without their intervention, the planes would have grown sideways as much as up, contemptuous of gravity, throwing out thick horizontal limbs for impossible distances. At the edge of the canopy, long twigs would droop down almost to the ground, louche and limp, like a prince's hand waiting for its courtier's kiss. One only has to look at the spreading arms of an unpruned plane to know why logs have knots. A branch does not begin at the edge of a trunk but at its very heart; it is the only way to stay up. A nail with its flat end glued to a wall would snap off as soon as touched, but drive it into a beam and it will hold a mirror four hundred times its own weight.

All Grove Park's plane trees bar one grow in the pavement. There is a single garden specimen at the front of No.18. The tree is of a similar age to those on the highway, but has grown differently. It avoided the Edwardian tree surgeons and branched early. Its centre of gravity is low, with thick limbs forming a goblet above a short trunk. Leaves from taller trees have decomposed in the bowl and dandelions, herb robert and thale cress grow happily – a little weedy mirror of the planted tree pits beyond the garden wall.

> Green is the plane-tree in the square,
> The other trees are brown;
> They droop and pine for country air;
> The plane-tree loves the town.

So wrote Amy Levy in 1889, the year she took her life. Levy was an early 'New Woman', a radical, independent, educated feminist, a twentieth-century ideal, like the motor car, living incongruously at the end of the Victorian era. For her the tree was a sign of resilience. It was unequivocally female and almost certainly symbolized the author herself:

Others the country take for choice,
And hold the town in scorn;
But she has listened to the voice
On city breezes borne.

Levy's plane tree thrives through yellow fog and grey smoke. It is a hopeful thing from a melancholy pen. For all their appearance of confidence and vigour, these trees too are vulnerable. In Europe they are developing open, oozing sores and dying of canker stain. The fungus behind the symptoms, *Ceratocystis platani*, evolved alongside the American plane, contentedly feeding on weak and damaged specimens of *Platanus occidentalis* and being gently repelled by those in good health. This is perfect parasitic behaviour – vigorously wiping out your host is a quick way to go extinct. However, humans have brought the fungus to the Old World and in the Oriental plane and the London plane, *Ceratocystis platani* has stumbled upon two species without defence. It is killing them without a thought for its own future. Let's hope it can be stopped in France, Italy, Greece and Switzerland, and that it never reaches Camberwell.

Not that we Southeast Londoners need any help to kill our plane trees. There may have been one hundred and twenty planted on Grove Park in 1865, but only half are left. Some will certainly have died in infancy when at their most vulnerable to drought and damage. But after reaching maturity any that have fallen have done so at the hands of man. Until the Great Storm of 1987, it was thought that plane trees could never blow over, and even in the face of that hurricane there were no losses on the Grove. Some of the fifty-nine missing trees were probably felled for developments – not every building on the street is late Victorian. Others were no doubt condemned as dangerous, leaning too far over the road, tipping towards the eaves of a house, or suffering some perceived or actual fault that might have increased our probability of being killed by a piece of falling tree, taking us from a one-in-ten-million chance to around one in 9,999,999.98.

Trees do rot, often invisibly and from the inside. Like humans they are both living and dead. Our lifeless tissue is always on show, it is our hair, nails and outer skin. Likewise, the majority of a tree's bark is dead – it grows from a thin band of cork cambium that functions like the cuticle on our fingernails. Below that is the phloem, living tissue that transports sugars and soluble nutrients. The next layer is made of undifferentiated cells that can move out to become phloem or inwards, to become xylem. If they make the move inwards they become part of the tree's plumbing. This is not an active job; water is attracted to water and it only travels in one direction: from the roots to the leaves. Individual molecules are links in a very weak chain. Each time a unit of $H_2O$ evaporates it drags the one behind into its place, which drags up the one behind, which drags up the one behind that and so on, all the way down to the tip of the roots. Living cells are full of bits that would obstruct this conga-line of liquid. What is needed is an inert tube. The xylem cells join up, lose their ends and die as a tiny part of a very long pipe.

When we count the rings on a tree, we are counting the number of pipes laid down in a year of growth. The inner rings no longer transport water. They have done their shift on the front line and are blocked with tannins and resin. They are now heartwood, with nothing to do but sit and help support the living bits for the remaining one hundred, three hundred, or two thousand years of the tree's life. That is, unless a pathogen gets in and begins to eat them. Fungus is the most common devourer of trees. A heavy blow with something solid – the end of a scaffold pole, for example, or a car in accidental reverse – can blow through the living layers and introduce spores of the wonderful *Fistulina hepatica,* the beefsteak fungus, or *Ganoderma australe,* the southern bracket, or *Laetiporus sulphureus*, the chicken of the woods, or any other of the hundreds of hollowing organisms.

This does not mean the end of the tree. All oak trees older than four hundred years are riddled with cavities and some are completely hollow, standing on sapwood alone, like an overcoat with nobody inside. There are holes in the plane trees of Grove Park. One has a pocket of decay high up on a horizontal limb. We on the street below would have no idea it was there, were there not a fairly large Torbay palm growing from it. *Cordyline australis* is not a true palm. It is a sword-leaved, branching tree from New Zealand, capable of reaching twenty metres and living for several hundred years. Some bird, I suspect the ring-necked parakeet, London's naturalized parrot, must have carried it up there in its gizzard. The plant is well into its third year of growth, and is I suspect the most horticulturally unique thing on the street. The branch that holds it might be rotten in places, but it survived the wind and leafed out again in spring, ready to spend another year serving as a lesson in the importance of looking up.

It took me days to find anything that had been seriously damaged by the storm. It seemed that all the drama of 5am had been for nothing. Finally, in Camberwell Old Cemetery, I found a silver maple that had blown apart in the gale. It was a huge old thing, a remnant of the cemetery's original nineteenth-century landscaping. A full third of the tree had been sundered from the trunk. The point of weakness was a vast outgrowth – a burr the size of a full-grown sheep – probably the result of some damage back when the tree was modest and human-sized. The fallen portion lay in fragments on the soft ground, every limb having shattered as if made of clay.

Several of the graves had been punctured and one old tomb lay demolished beneath the wreckage. Its resident, Albert Helps, had been laid to rest in 1892 at the age of sixty-six. He would have been buried near a slender young tree with green leaves that flashed silver in the breeze. How different from Robert Blair's churchyard yew, that 'Cheerless unsocial plant! that loves to dwell / 'Midst skulls and coffins, epitaphs and worms.' None of the mourners could have suspected that the bright young maple would one day drop a massive carbuncled limb onto their beloved's place of eternal rest.

I went back to the broken tree on a grey day in the first week of January. The wood still pressed hard on the ruined stone but it was covered in cotton balls of white and red. Even severed from the roots the buds had opened and after one hundred and thirty years, fresh flowers decked the grave of Albert Helps, who is that rarest of things: a Londoner truly connected with the city soil.

# 11

# CAMELLIA

The last day of the year was cold. At the end of my road, Goose Green froze solid behind its low hoop-top railings. The park was not rimed in silver and made no attempt to glitter, sparkle, charm or otherwise beguile. It was churned mud, as it had been the week before, only now it was harder. The dog walkers were still in their houses when Solomon and I passed through, but we were able to bump across their solidified boot prints to visit trees that had been marooned in sludge for over a month. It was exiting to be on this temporary ground. We marched like a Swedish army on a frosted sea, off to fight the Danes.

Up on Grove Park, a man a few years older than me was balanced on top of his recycling bin, ankle-deep in layers of wrapping paper and cardboard. He was in a breakfast outfit, an old blue T-shirt and checked pyjama trousers. From where I stood in my boots and coat he looked soft and vulnerable, like a baby bird out of its nest and cooling fast. I had an urge to shoo him inside, to tell him to get back in the warm. I would squash in the Lego boxes.

It is no great surprise that being a parent evokes parental feelings, but this was oddly indiscriminate. The man lived in a bigger house than mine on a nicer, wider road. He was successful, his family had received many presents and he did not need a slightly younger gardener to be his daddy. But I was finding it increasingly hard to see anybody in distress, from the sprawled drunk to the teased schoolboy, without imagining that it could one day be my son. I could no longer bear to see someone cold. We trundled on and saw the first of the street camellias in flower.

The flowers of *Camellia japonica* are large and velutinous. Draw a thumbnail across a petal and it will bruise and brown. When we were little, my brother, sister and I used *Camellia japonica* as the main ingredient in our potions and homemade perfumes. The flowers were beautiful and could be mashed into a disgusting gunk, a symbolic and powerful transformation. The scents we tried to manufacture were never a success. Andrew Cavendish, the 11th Duke of Devonshire, could have explained why. He once told the *Daily Telegraph*: 'If I may be bossy enough to give you a good tip, my dear, it is that you can always tell a non-gardener by someone who smells a camellia. Because they don't smell.' The Duke was, of course, wrong. Many of the *sasanqua* camellias are highly fragrant, but they did not grow in our childhood garden, nor, it seems, at Chatsworth House.

The Grove Park camellia was a *japonica*, and truly scentless. It was also a sparse and leaning thing, with the pale wood of its stem visible through its glossy green leaves. But that's how I like my camellias. Not for me the perfectly rounded bush with its foliage to the ground and all the elegance of a cheese dome, as if a set designer has slung roses at a blob of laurel. No, bare and twisted camellias are true to the ancient Chinese and Japanese paintings of the plant by which it was first introduced to us Europeans. Zhou Shuxi's *Camellia and a Lonely Bird*, painted in the late seventeenth century, features a branch so naked and meagre that it would be pruned off and burned in a modern botanical garden. Utagawa Hiroshige, the last great master of Ukiyo-e painting, obsessively composed stylized images of the warbling white-eye bird perched on a red-flowered camellia. Sometimes the plant is in snow, sometimes in sun, but it always looks as if a passerby has pulled off most of its leaves.

And perhaps they had. Camellias are a famine food. Zhu Su, a prince of the Ming Dynasty, includes it in his *Jiuhuang Bencao*, which can be roughly translated as 'Treatise on Wild Food Plants for Use in Emergency'. No modern forager's guide has bettered this work of 1406. Richard Mabey's constantly revised classic, *Food for Free*, contains two hundred edibles, Zhu Su identified four hundred and fourteen. For *Camellia japonica* he recommends briefly cleaning the leaves before boiling them and tossing with oil and salt. I thought it unfair to pull the leaves from the Grove Park camellia and so used sprigs harvested from work when testing this recipe. I chose fresh growth; not the dark, shining, mature leaves, but little ones the colour of frozen peas. The oil and salt do most of the lifting and the taste is bitter, but not as lingering as one might expect. As a side dish they would be overwhelming but they might work if blanched and deep-fried like a sage crisp and served with ice-cold beer.

Europe's first camellias were certainly not for eating. They were precious things grown under glass by proud owners. Richard Folkard tells the story of their introduction in his six-hundred-page compendium *Plant Lore, Legends, and Lyrics*. They arrived from the Far East with Georg Joseph Kamel, the Jesuit after which the genus is named. On landing in Spain, the missionary hurried to the palace, securing an immediate audience with Queen Maria Theresa. He was ushered into the royal chambers cradling the shrub in a mother-of-pearl vase. It had two perfect white flowers. The Queen was overcome. She plucked a bloom, ran straight to the King and embraced him, shouting 'Behold the new flower of the Philippines!'

As an origin tale it is fitting but false. Queens rarely entertain ship-stained Jesuits; dysentery killed Georg Joseph Kamel in Manila before he could return; and *Camellia japonica* is not found in the Philippines. Its introduction to the British Isles is the more usual tale of East India trading ship meets English aristocrat. By 1739, it was growing in Lord Petre of Thorndon Hall's collection. He died three years later at the age of twenty-nine, leaving a private nursery of 219,925 plants, some of which travelled with his head gardener, James Gordon, to a new commercial enterprise in London's Mile End, from where the camellia began its invasion of England.

As something both formal and florid, the camellia was made for the Victorians. In their extensive floriography it came to symbolize either perfected beauty, admiration or longing, depending on which author was pulling it all out of thin air that day. William Roscoe, the son of a market gardener who became by turn banker, abolitionist, member of parliament and poet, wrote of a contest between the goddesses Venus and

Diana. Venus plucked a musk rose from its dew-bent spray and showered it with her scent, enough to steal the soul of the virgin huntress Diana and convince her that seduction holds more power than the drawn bow. But Diana replied, with a severe smile, 'Be others by thy amorous arts beguiled' for her favourite flower was the chaste camellia, whose pure and spotless bloom boasts no fragrance and conceals no thorn.

Of course it is paradoxical to have any flower represent chastity. They are all sex organs, some of them as monstrously oversized and cartoonish as any on the internet. As an ornamental species, *Camellia japonica* suffers from exaggerated blooms. There are many outlandishly petalled cultivars on the market, all of them created by plant breeders. In these, the glorious golden nest of filament-floated stamens has been replaced by more petals, creating a ruffled sphere like an exfoliating shower scrunchie. This means no pollen, but it also means no access to pollen for the buried female parts. The lack of a functioning stigma and style ensures the ovaries remain empty and the hormonal message 'I'm fertilized, drop the petals' is forever unsent. This leads to the camellia's much-criticized tendency to retain its spent blooms and greet the summer hung in brown tissue, looking for all the world like a sewer flood's tragic survivor.

It is unfair to do this to a noble shrub, particularly as its symbolic power in Japan lies largely in the tumbling moment when a fertilized flower drops whole and perfect to the forest floor. A poet of the Edo period named Yosa Buson celebrated gravity's sudden intrusion into a still garden with the haiku 'A camellia falls, spilling out rain water from yesterday'. It is worth eulogizing because most flowers drop petal by petal; think of cherry blossom carried on a spring breeze. The camellia's split-second slip from perfect life to abrupt death is beautiful and sinister. It was revered by the samurai who glimpsed a hundred honourable beheadings in each shrub. Perhaps this is why it plays a part in Kurosawa's magnificent film *Sanjuro*, in which the samurai's brutal attack is triggered by camellia flowers floating downstream from the villains' compound.

The Reverend Robert Tyas published a language of flowers in 1842. It has nearly everything required to let the bouquet do the talking. To say 'your qualities surpass your charms', give mignonette. For sorrowful remembrances, give red chamomile or, if things are beyond redemption, use asphodel for 'my regrets follow you to the grave'. Use spring's primrose to suggest early youth and autumn's crocus to say 'my best days are past'. If the news is bad, break it with a mulberry tree, which means 'I will not survive you'. An unappreciated artist might be given coltsfoot with the comfort that justice will be done to you, the next age will see the truth of your work, even if this one cannot. *Rosa lutea*, the yellow rose, is for infidelity, almond trees for mere indiscretion. The snowdrop is consolation and borage bluntness. However, there is no flower to say 'I am currently menstruating and will service you when I am finished.' For that the world would have to wait six years while Alexandre Dumas *fils* had his affair with Marie Duplessis and took the time to novelize it.

Of course, nowhere in *La Dame aux Camélias* is the meaning of the flowers carried by the beautiful courtesan Marguerite Gautier explicitly stated. Even for *le bohème* Paris, that would have been risqué. But when she sits at every opening night with a bunch of camellias, white for twenty-five days, then red for five, then back to white, are we to believe the narrator when he says that no one knows why? Or do we give a knowing wink when he says that he only *mentions* it, he can't *explain* it. Today we know Gautier better as Violetta Valéry from Verdi's *La Traviata* and everyone who walks, drives or lives on Grove Park will be familiar with her allegretto call to 'yield to temptation', if not from the opera then from adverts for Dutch beer or crisps.

Whether passersby associate December's last frozen bloom with that doomed heroine, or with the samurai, or with childhood potions, risible Victorians, sewer floods or anything else, depends on the viewer's lived experience and their willingness to actively distinguish a plant from its neighbour. But for a few people, willingness does not come into it. They have camellias indelibly seared on their brains and could not hope to walk the pavement by No.87 without being taken back, boats against the current, to some other place in some other time.

I am carried six Januarys into the past and eight miles to the west, to Chiswick House in the run-up to the great Camellia Festival. I was working there in a mid-ranking, muddy-fingered sort of role. I drove an electric buggy with a bin full of spades and secateurs round the overgrown residue of the place where William Kent 'leaped the fence, and saw that all nature was a garden'. There, from the 1730s, the great painter-turned-garden-designer built an Arcadia with wiggly edges and arguably birthed the English Landscape Movement, Capability Brown and all. Under my tenure it was no longer an aristocratic pleasure ground but a heavily templed public park. Still romantic, charmed, impressive and wild. Lord Burlington's bowling green was by then a churned clearing in heavy woods. The sweet chestnuts planted as slender columns had heaved and sunk the ground until it rolled like harpooned whales under a brown tarpaulin. Any bowl aimed on their flanks would swerve and dip were it not for the thick mud sticking it in place as soon as it landed.

The Palladian villa survives from Burlington's day, as do the Ionic Temple, the Amphitheatre and the Obelisk. The Grade-I-listed conservatory is a later addition – three hundred feet of constantly rotting and ever-repaired glass and white-painted wood. The Beatles filmed their video for *Paperback Writer* there, not bringing a drum kit so while the others play guitar, Ringo forever sits on the mosaic floor and nods. The whole thing was built in the early nineteenth century for hothouse fruit, but in 1828 the 6th Duke of Devonshire, a man who esteemed beauty over figs, converted it into two giant camellia beds. It is now the oldest collection of indoor camellias in Europe. Each February, they stand in the public gaze for the annual Camellia Festival – an event that takes eleven months of pruning, feeding, watering and weeding to deliver.

Under the glass the camellias were always content. They would have been happier a few yards away beneath the open sky, but they never suffered any frost damage. The real benefactors of the greenhouse, of *any* greenhouse, were the fungi. There was no wind and no cold. The aisles were wet with vegetable respiration. The plants, stones, workers and wood were rocks in a sea-fog of vapour and spore. Aphids flourished. Each shrub's spring growth fed multitudes, all safe from the blue tits and the ladybirds outside. Aphids leak. Their sweet exudate coated everything. Bruised raspberries could not have gone off quicker than those sugary leaves in the humid air. A month before the great festival and each one was crusted with sooty mould.

I worked solidly while winter threw itself against the glass. One afternoon was dark with thick snow capping the sloping panes. Other days were bright with spring sunshine, the fragrance of jonquil daffodils blooming in pots on the stone benches. Sometimes the garden volunteers joined me. Occasionally my horticultural trainee worked nearby. With buckets of warm water we cleaned every leaf. Each mouldy surface was lightless, matt and oven-tray black, but with a forefinger curled below and a thumb-rub on top they became suddenly clean and glorious. The plant cells were untouched, the waxy cuticle all the shinier for its buffing. Each reclaimed lamina was a victory, each branch a small miracle. The first polished plant shone next to its neighbours like glittering virtue in Hell's third circle, or the 'after' smile in a dentist's brochure.

This is what I see when I see a camellia. I look at leaves before the bloom. And when they are glossy and perfect, I feel a shiver of satisfaction that is somehow a part of my brain.

Another person involuntarily triggered by camellias is Monty Don. The man is an excellent television presenter, but is perhaps better as a garden writer. In an article for the *Guardian* he confesses to an ingrained prejudice against camellias, heathers, miniature conifers and rhododendrons – not on grounds of taste, we must understand, but geography. His hated school was on acid soil, his home on alkaline, so as the beech trees faded and the monkey puzzles loomed, his youthful little bones knew that the dread place drew nearer.

It is a very good excuse for disliking a deeply unfashionable group of shrubs. Harold Nicolson, husband of Vita Sackville-West and progenitor of roughly half of Sissinghurst's genius, also loathed most ericaceous plants, though he did not blame it on his love for the chalky Kentish soil. In response to one of Vita's inspired planting plans, he called azaleas 'Sunningdale sort of plants', not fitting for 'our lovely romantic Saxon, Roman, Tudor, Kent', and added that anything with the suggestion of suburbia should be avoided. He was even better on rhododendrons, comparing them to 'large stock-brokers whom we do not want to have to dinner'. How I wish he had written a gardening book to sit aside his biographies of Swinburne and the many histories of diplomacy.

The man balanced on the bin might well have been a stockbroker, he certainly had the house for it; but I didn't despise him, in fact I felt a fleeting sort of love for him. Perhaps because I don't know any stockbrokers, I haven't developed the synaptic path allowing me to see one and think 'bad dinner party'. Harold had, and his life was different for it. We all see the world through a lens of experience. My camellia is different from your camellia, even if they are both the bare and wonky one growing outside No.87. If you are reading this and thinking, 'But I have no instinctive camellia associations', then go and make some. Take bus 176 to Camberwell Green and walk up the hill to Grove Park. There's the one you've been reading about at 87, but also a low bushy number at 91, three in a row at No.59, hard on the pavement. There are two at No.4 and one at No.3, looking distinguished and handsome between a high hedge and ivy-clad trellis. No.54 has a huge bulky one beside the door like a bouncer. No.44 has at least two and 41 just one, but it comes out early, sometimes by Christmas, if you are in need of a gift for yourself.

# 12

# GRAPEVINE

Frozen air blew east at the North Pole while we celebrated Christmas. Up there, far from Grove Park and the first camellias of spring, the sun did not rise for months and there was only black between the sea-ice and the stars. Unseen, the wind chased itself through the dark, while South London tentatively went out jogging, until the end of January when the vortex fragmented. Bits of it eddied off over Yakutsk, Greenland and the Bering Sea. The jet stream's girdle slackened and a numbing bulge of Nordic troposphere crept down towards Camberwell.

By the second week of February it had reached us. At work, the ground froze hard and my spade scratched lines on the soil. I was building a fernery on the edge of some woodland. The rocks were in place but the loam and leafmould were bagged in one-ton cubes, now solid, white-topped and unworkable. I gave up and cycled home over polished snow, one hand tucked into the crook of my arm to keep the pinch from my fingers.

Sol was serving a two-day suspension from nursery for a funny tummy. He was fine, up on his feet by now and staggering destructively around the flat, exploring the different climate zones: the cold by the bay window, the warm pool of the radiator, the thin draught under the back door. It was wrong to be needlessly pumping heat through the cracks in the house so we turned down the boiler, wrapped up warm and went outside.

In William Black's 1876 novel *Madcap Violet* there is a description of Grove Park before the houses came. Violet North visits friends in Camberwell, having spent two years away. After an evening of talk she steels herself to raise the question she fears most: 'I am almost afraid to ask it,' she says. 'Have they built over Grove Park yet?' 'Certainly not,' comes the answer. 'And the cedars are still there, and the tall elms, and the rooks' nests?' she gasps. Could it be true? With hungry London growing ever-closer. Yes, Violet, they assure her, 'not a thing altered since you left'.

Violet melts. She talks of her memories, of night-time silence in the meadows, up close to the heavens, with nothing about but white snow and black trees. She says it was the most beautiful place she could possibly remember.

But where *is* it? asks young Miller. Somewhere in Camberwell? *That* is the most beautiful place you can remember? And you have been to *Chamounix*?

She has been to Chamonix! But perhaps George Miller has not been to Grove Park? It is rectified there and then. They walk beneath the cedars and weep at the view to Sydenham. George Miller concedes that Chamonix has been destroyed, Mont Blanc has been ground to dust, the Glacier des Bossons is no more. It is *all* Camberwell now.

If I met Violet today, would I too thrill as her shawl brushed my glove? Maybe, but things would progress no further. She would run as soon as I conceded that, 'Yes, they built over Grove Park, but there's now a good wisteria at 91. I've written a book about it.'

At least my son and I could still experience the snow. Up there the pavements were not salted. They remained white, while those on Bellenden Road were pink and pocked with grit. I lifted Solomon from his pram and let him make tiny footprints. In 1895 a Camberwell School master named John B Coppock proposed that snow cleaned the air by acting as a diffuse filter. He collected samples from four inches that covered the suburb on the 13th of January, melted them and found eleven polluting grains per gallon of water, around half of them being soot. Most of the particles came from the bottom two inches of snow, indicating that the air got cleaner as the snow fell through it. We did not have four inches, but then, we did not have the soot levels of 1895, and I let the baby eat as much as he liked.

On the boundary between 34 and 35, he broke free, turning without warning and walking a few steps down the garden path. He stopped, transfixed by a thin brown twig between the railings. It looked like a root, out of place above the soil, hung on the bars as a warning to other plants. I took my second-ever step into a Grove Park garden and with one of his tiny hands in mine, began to guide him out. But the twig had seized his whole attention. As his body moved left, his head turned right until he was staring over one shoulder. In danger of losing sight of the little stick, he let his legs liquefy under him and was dragged out dangling from my arm like a teddy being bumped upstairs to bed.

It is the twig that is important here, not the drag marks in the snow. It was the finest, thinnest part of a grapevine. I had been watching it from stump to tendril for almost a full year and was pleased to see it snag Solomon's flickering curiosity. *Vitis* on a suburban street is unusual. Goodness knows why – the search for a better front garden plant would be a long one. Vines are drought-tolerant and attractive in all seasons. They are productive and, above all, pliant. These are trees made liquid. Like an epoxy resin, they have a malleable, flowing state that sets hard and strong. In Andalusian towns they are trained over the alleys, turning streets into green-lit tunnels, their gnarled trunks against the houses, their fresh leaves against the sky. Why can't we have that in Southeast London?

Like those in Cadiz, the grapevine at No.34 was both old and young. Plants are not like us, with all our organs ageing in step, our livers as old as our lungs, our heart-span as long as our head-span. Humans display determinate growth. All being well, we reach the proper size for our species and then we stop. Vines exhibit indeterminate growth. Given the right conditions, new leaves, stems and roots can be generated almost indefinitely – an ancient forearm sprouts fingers, an elbow resting on the ground grows toes.

A pruned vine renews yearly from a twisted framework. It is a miracle of growth. A thing that might have been made of cast iron, beads with green, like a spike driven through the earth into a pressurized vat of emerald goo. Life is extruded from buds in the black wood, stretching fast and thin towards the light as the world wakes. In their first season, these are shoots. When winter has taken their leaves and browned their bark, we call them canes. Unpruned, a cane begins to thicken into a trunk or branch, though unless the vine's bone structure wants changing, all will be cut away in the cold months of dormancy. New stems flower in early summer and fruit in the autumn. We want lots. It is the plant's primary growth method, the only way of reaching sun and support wires, and of bearing new things like leaves and grapes. But there is also secondary growth, an annual all-over thickening, that sees the plant lay on cells in cambium layers beneath the skin of old wood. Each hoop of tissue is a tree ring in the stem and a miniature act of gnarling in the bark. Add a few decades of them together and a shoot becomes a cudgel and a cane becomes a thick arm, bud-studded and pregnant with next season's stems.

The vine at No.34 is stretching its arms. Each autumn a cane towards the outer limit is tied to the railing's top when the others are pruned off; the end of this was what caught Solomon's eye. One day it will not look like a new segment, it will be an indistinguishable part of a thick and fissured horizontal trunk that could have been squeezed evenly onto the metal from a car-sized toothpaste tube. No.34 is one of the only gardens on Grove Park with railings. It is long and overcrowded with fruit trees, as though an orchard has been corralled. Without doubt it is one of my favourite gardens on the road. I like the exuberance, the 'I'll have it all, and another plum tree in the corner' nature of the planting. It is a garden where things have been put in because they were desired, not just because there was space to fill. But mostly I like it for the ironwork and the vine.

London railings and climbing plants were meant for each other. Together they are a distillation of the rigid-structure-with-vegetable-fluff ideal that is the heart of a great garden. The vertical balusters suck growth upwards. It's because they are thin. Anyone who has sent a clematis to scrabble uselessly against the fat, smooth, trunk of an apple tree will know that girth is the climber's enemy. Grapes evolved to exploit the trailing outer branches of bigger shrubs. They take their wood skinny and their metal the same way, even a drainpipe is too thick. Once the top rail is reached and there's nowhere left to climb, the plant switches its attention to lying on structural wood. For this, something long, strong and solid is required.

Fences won't work. They understand that at No.34. Wooden or wire structures are ungainly when covered in growth. They are too temporary. A wall can support a rose without inducing nervousness because we know the brick and mortar will live as long as the plant. Larchlap and cedar slats, on the other hand, can only rot and this knowledge nags at the petals and cheapens the whole thing. Flowering railings have it the right way round – the structure is eternal, the beauty ephemeral. And no matter how twiggy the top growth, the spiked finials of the railing heads give the forbearing dignity of architecture under siege.

In October I plucked a single berry from a dark cluster hidden under the reddening leaves. It tasted like a wine grape; thick chewy skin, sweet but high in tannins and full of seed, very different from the crisp, refrigerated flavour of a supermarket's table grape. It would be possible to make a bottle or two from the fruit at No.34. Not so long ago it was common to harvest and press grapes in cottage gardens smaller than the one Solomon had staggered into. Vita Sackville-West saw the phenomenon as a sad relic of a once-noble vintager tradition, writing in her *New Statesman* column: 'Here and there a solitary vine exists to provide its bunches annually, which in due course are turned into an excruciatingly nasty drink labelled "Homemade wine" by cottage-wives.'

She was writing for 'Country Notes', a fortnightly dispatch from the nut woods of Sissinghurst that ran in 1938 and 1939 – rural relief from the impending war and Churchill's promises that the British would 'go down fighting'. What balm to turn the page on that close-lined newsprint, to leave Germany's rearmament behind and slip into a green world with Vita. 'We, who live in Kent, do not forget about it and have no wish to do so,' begins one article. 'This is a countryside that needs knowing. It needs a close and loving knowledge of the lanes, the villages, the changes of light, and the lost places.'

Were Vita reincarnated, or better yet, if she had never died, if she lived on as Orlando, her sex-shifting avatar from Virginia Woolf's novel, would she still believe Kent worth knowing? I think so. To see her beloved hills as they now are, the heart of an exciting new wine region, would thrill her. She knew that the North Downs had once boasted vineyards because, of course, she had read their audit in the Domesday Book. But she was writing just two generations from the end of Britain's miniature ice age and still saw the heavy soil ('that yellow enemy') as too cold for grapes.

In her magisterial book-length poem *The Land*, she describes the making of beer and cider – small steps in the farmer's year-long dance. Hop-drying is rough and industrial, its heat is from the furnace, not the field. It takes coal to stoke the kilns, and when the oven doors are shut, the shovelling men sit and play at dice (and swear, and spit, and grumble at the price). Cider, meanwhile, is the pressing of a cold country:

And sharp like no rich southern wine
The tang of cider bites;
For here the splintered stars and hard
Hold England in a frosty guard

But wine is a different drink, as ancient and pagan as the sun. *The Land* ends with the recollection of another harvest, beneath another sky. Not Kent's ('so Saxon-fair, so washed by dews and rain') but in an older place where gods wake at evenfall and 'the dusk is heavy with the wine's warm load'. There waits Virgil, her acknowledged inspiration; a man who toiled with his stylus, 'shy as a peasant in the Courts of Rome', and still took time to love the rose. With the poet she watches the purple stain of the grapes spread in wagons from the hills. Vita was a sherry drinker (and Juliet Nicolson writes of her grandmother being wheelbarrowed from the flower beds by discreet gardeners). We can't know if she would enjoy the crisp whites now produced around Sissinghurst, but how she would relish seeing the harvest swing home down a Kentish lane.

My favourite vine is not grown for grapes. *Vitis coignetiae* is a leaf-man's plant. Each one is as large as a plate, blunt and round like a brontosaur's footprint. They stack and overlap, covering walls and pergolas with scales of brilliant green that turn unguessably to yellow, red and burgundy each autumn. It is the most vigorous *Vitis* in existence. One would do for four or five Grove Park gardens. The thing was brought to Europe by Madame Coignet, who picked it up while travelling in Japan. Back in France the vines were dying, punctured a million billion times by the needle-mouth of the American *Phylloxera* aphid. Noble grape varieties went extinct. There was a real possibility that workers would have to drink fermented sugar beet and *la classe moyenne* learn to enjoy whisky and soda. Madame Coignet's vine was sent to vineyards and scientific institutions in the hope that its vitality could save wine. It did not work – grafted Texan rootstocks did the job instead – but so many visitors to *l'École Nationale Supérieure d'Horticulture* remarked, 'My God, what is it?', that 'it', *Vitis coignetiae*, became an ornamental plant.

My first encounter was in London's Regent's Park. I was on a day trip with classmates, all of us studying for our Business and Technology Education Council Certificate in Horticulture. We had spent the first part of the week learning to clean lawnmower sparkplugs in a temporary classroom by the A406, but had been released in central London for the 'Principles of Garden Design' module. It was late summer. We were in the garden of

St John's Lodge at the dead-centre of the park and the vine was still sending out fresh green tendrils, even as other strands were blooded with end-of-year red. It had covered a steel pergola and now lounged there massively. Through arches below, the calm lawn and grey benches of the Oval Garden could be seen. It was enough to make us young students think, 'Who needs principles of garden design? Give us something uncontrolled and wild with something cool and clipped beyond. We know it all now, so send us back to the machinery shed.'

If, like me, they stayed in gardening, my contemporaries will have fixed a lot of lawnmowers by now, but I doubt they will have done any serious vine-work. I certainly haven't, though it used to be one of the core skills of the ambitious head gardener, a tangible way to demonstrate expertise and worth. The grape bench at a Victorian horticultural show was their place of battle. Henry Bright, author of *The English Flower Garden* (1881), found himself flustered by this peacocking from the servant class, writing:

Nothing can be more spoiling to the gardener than these flower-shows. In the first place, the prize-ticket generally asserts that the prize is adjudged to 'Mr —, gardener to —'. The owner of the garden is nobody, and the gardener is everything. The prize is in almost every case regarded as the unchallenged property of the gardener, who has, nevertheless, won the prize by his master's plant, reared at his master's expense.

Bright would approve of the last celebrated grape duel. It was fought between Andrew Cavendish, 11th Duke of Devonshire (seen earlier asserting that camellias have no smell), and the 11th Duke of Marlborough, John Spencer-Churchill. Their arena was Vincent Square in London, home of the Royal Horticultural Society and its annual Harvest Festival. In breathless reports from the 1990s and 2000s, the press did their best to imply that His Grace the Duke of Devonshire had been out spraying Bordeaux mixture, a fungicide, while His Grace the Duke of Marlborough spent freezing afternoons hewing at extension growth. In the quest for First Place Table Grape, no salaried gardener was ever mentioned.

Outside commercial vineyards there remains one prestigious position in horticultural viticulture: Keeper of the Great Vine at Hampton Court Palace. The role is dedicated to the upkeep and optimization of what is recognized as the world's largest grapevine, a two-hundred-and-fiftty-year-old woodheap in the corner of a specially built glasshouse. The plant is worth a visit; its trunk is almost four metres round, though this was not enough for a teenager on my last visit. 'Is that it?' she complained. Her mother asked what she expected, and the girl said she thought it might be a mile long or something.

She would find the Grove Park vine a disappointment – it's barely twelve feet from tip to tip. Solomon has lost interest in it completely and there is no way Violet North would take it as compensation for the loss of her cedar trees. But show it to me, wrapped around the black railings and burning with autumn fire, and I will happily tell you that it is the most beautiful twelve feet this side of Chamonix.

# 13

## TULIP

At work we pruned the orchard in January. It was a mid-winter job and the sun could barely be bothered to look. Each day it put in its token appearance, slicing over the horizon, obligated to show up but clearly longing to be back over the Southern Hemisphere, beating down on Chilean vineyards and the mangoes of Jakarta. It's hard not to think of such places when one's hands are frozen in a hook around the handle of a saw. With the new baby at home I was seeing more night than ever before, sometimes up three or four hours before the sky had begun to yellow. On the estate, we gardeners had been given a Portakabin toilet to use while our mess room was dismantled. It had needle-sharp strip lights and in the mirror my eyes sat in wrinkled semi-circles of shadowy blue.

Gardeners are quick to gnarl. We live in the wind and ultraviolet. My lips and hands crack every time the temperature drops. And I smile a lot, which has driven crinkle lines across my face. One afternoon I looked at myself after a shift on the ladder, my cheek pressed to an apple trunk, and thought, that man is developing quite an interesting patina. It was a piece of fatigue-induced disassociation. I am normally as vain as the next person, but it was nice to look at my skin as if it were bark, with all the marks and patterns welcomed as character.

In the depths of winter, Grove Park felt distant. I sometimes cycled through on my way home. The gardens were private and black. Standing at the fence looking in at 5pm was as rewarding as at midnight, and equally as sinister. I felt grateful to the families who had strung golden Christmas lights through their potted olive trees, but it was clear that I would only be able to commune with the other plants in permitted daylight hours. I had become a weekend dad, always struggling to reacquaint myself, missing the moments of development and only seeing the results. Snowdrops flowering in a tree pit by No.85 surprised me. I had missed the moment they broke through the surface, their two leaves clasped over a single scape, like a diver in reverse, hands out in front, palm to palm, ready to part the water. I had later missed the green blades separating, growing out and away from the vertical bud in its protective spathe. I missed the upward unwrapping of the flower's sheaf and, a day or so later, three inches from the ground, I missed the neck bend that brought it down into the classic pearl-earring hang. Instead I walked past and thought: a snowdrop, how nice. I had lost out on the thrill of anticipation, robbed by the tilt of the earth and by Greenwich Mean Time with its insistence that mornings get the most of the winter light. It didn't matter that my work had me out in snowdrop meadows all week and that I had seen five hundred thousand of the little things pushing their way up over the previous month. I had not been there as the first snowdrop on Grove Park grew up and, silly as it seems, that was rather painful.

For observers of other people's gardens, tulips are a better flower. Their rise starts in the gloomy afternoons of early March, but it is April when they bud. By then the clocks have gone forward, we can take walks while dinner cooks and add botanical loops to our commutes. Flower-watching season begins. 'Guess the tulip' is a fun game to play. There is a garden I pass on the way to Dulwich Park. It has black and white tiles in a classic chequerboard pattern. A line of box separates these from an expanse of slate chips and three lollipop bay trees in a perfect line. It is faultlessly formal. The seasons flow round it.

After rain, the path is shiny and I have twice seen snow cover the slate, otherwise it is endlessly unchanging. Or it was until last year when the stone chips were pushed away from the topiary and each one sprouted a skirt of tulip leaves. I guessed *Tulipa* 'Spring Green', the classic Viridiflora tulip, cream with a tasteful peeled-cucumber stripe up each petal. But no, they came out brilliantly and brutally orange. And not an elegant, Lily-flowered orange like *Tulipa* 'Ballerina'. These were vast tumbler-sized blooms from the Darwin Hybrid group, the height and colour of a motorway traffic cone. I adored them and laughed out loud when they opened. To me they sat in the same category as a letter of resignation or a new tattoo – small signs of a Londoner saying bollocks to it all.

Lily-flowered, Viridiflora and Darwin Hybrid are three of the fifteen divisions into which commercially available tulips are placed. The others are: Single Early (short, sturdy and March-flowering here in Camberwell), Double Early (ruffled, mid-season, long-lasting), Triumph (breeder's favourite, spectrum-spanning colours from mid-April), Single Late (tall, old-fashioned, aristocratic), Fringed (petals like ripped velvet), Rembrandt (beautifully virus-mottled, see the still-life paintings of the eponymous master), Parrot (buds like the closed jaws of a crocodile, oil-spill petals), Double Late (huge, puffy pompoms), Kaufmanniana (small and well-hinged, opening into a six-pointed star), Fosteriana (large flowers on short stems), Greigii (dense petals, leaves mottled like the flanks of a cellar slug) and Species (any of the seventy or so wild species offered for sale). Lily-flowered tulips are cinch-waisted and flick-topped, shaped like a scrawl in a stylist's notebook. Viridifloras have green-tinged petals (viridian is pushing it) and Darwin Hybrids are a spilled bucket of Fosteriana and *Tulipa gesneriana* DNA, all mopped up and poured into a bulb of exceptional vigour and longevity.

Each of these tulips has its place in the garden, and that place, in my opinion, is among the foliage of other plants. Unless set out in tight ranks as spring bedding, they do not have enough leaf to carry a skirt of bare earth, certainly not in a small front garden where space is limited. Snowdrops can do it. They have two long blades for each small flower and provide their own green background. Admittedly, they have the advantage of rising when the year is newborn and anything living is prized; and they emerge against January soil, which is generally dark, wet and black. April is a month of desiccating wind. Even when the water table is high, the ground can appear cracked and chapped. This is not a health problem for tulips, they are natives of the Central Asian tablelands and no spring in England could ever be too dry, it is an aesthetic one – it upsets the eye of the observer. I don't like to see something so lush and fresh as a tulip above ground that looks like crispy bran flakes.

Even above moist soil, tulips can look ill proportioned and out of place. Tall daffodils suffer from the same problem before they form clumps. There is too much up and not enough out. They are church spires without transepts, mountains without foothills. These plants need to break from a green sea to look comfortable. The emerging foliage of herbaceous perennials is good. Hardy geraniums, euphorbias and wallflowers work well. Another path is to pair them with classic spring flowers, a hazy mat of blue forget-me-nots (*Myosotis sylvatica*), purple honesty (*Lunaria annua*) and domes of clotted-cream primroses (*Primula vulgaris*). I like to grow tulips in unmown lawn. By the time they come into flower the grass is perfectly tufty, long enough to look romantic, short enough to stand up under heavy dew. The tulips should be accompanied by as many other types of bulbs as can be stomached. Snowdrops, of course, which will be long green mop-tops by tulip time, but also their later-flowering cousin, the knee-high summer snowflake (*Leucojum vernum*). There should also be daffodils; dwarfs for February, taller ones for March and April, with a mixture of single and multi-headed types, some in the colour of orange squash, others in that of pale barley water. Certainly some muscari; the broad-leaved type (*Muscari latifolium*) is neater but it doesn't really matter because rough grass will mask the scribbling foliage of the common grape hyacinth (*Muscari neglectum*). Wood anemones (*Anemone nemorosa*) should be allowed to clump, their deep-cut leaves providing relief to all the straps and spikes sent up by the bulbs. I like the pale blue cultivar 'Robinsoniana' but common white will be lovely. These will need cover from the summer sun so it's worth throwing a few deciduous trees over the whole lot – magnolias maybe, perhaps a spreading cornus, or even a classic hazel copse as seen in Sissinghurst's Nuttery and Gertrude Jekyll's Primrose Garden. And there you have it – that's how to plant a tulip.

Of course this approach is the antithesis of how tulips have been treated for most of their thousand-year history of cultivation. These were expensive curios, to be enjoyed like jewels in a display case. Most people have heard of the Dutch Republic's famous 'tulip mania' of 1635–7, when contracts for theoretical future ownership of bulbs changed hands at ludicrously speculative prices. Charles Mackay brought the story to a vast audience with his 1841 book *Extraordinary Popular Delusions and the Madness of Crowds* and reports one trader offering twelve acres of land for a single virus-mottled bulb of 'Semper Augustus'. But if Mackay is to be believed, and that is in some doubt, then the sums paid were for financial instruments that were only nominally related to the bulbiferous plant. After the bubble popped, the tulips' price realigned with its value to the gardener but prized specimens remained vastly too costly for the average citizen. Anna Pavord's excellent history *The Tulip* tells the story of this bulb in brilliantly exhaustive detail, and is stuffed with aristocrats, cardinals, kings, princes, sultans and grand vizirs, many as exotic as the plants they coveted. These were the people who could afford to exchange the rarest tulip bulbs and who did so with a passion that could override political convictions, turning battlefield enemies into brothers. Pavord tells the story of Sir Thomas Hanmer, a royalist baronet and cupbearer to Charles I, who, in June 1655, with the English Civil War just finished and the land under the rule of Oliver Cromwell, sent a root of his prized bulb 'Agate Hanmer' to Major General John Lambert, the great Parliamentarian war hero. This was not an act of tribute but a connoisseur wishing to share his passion with a like-minded devotee.

In the 1650s, both Roundheads and Cavaliers would have planted their tulips the same way – in measured rows with clear space between each. There were to be no distractions from the flower and certainly no muscari or wood anemones to get in the way and fuzz things up. This was a flower to be looked down upon from above and appreciated for its tiny parts: the petals, anthers and markings at the base of each cup. But fashions change. In the eighteenth century, England's wealthy tastemakers dug up and grassed over their treasure gardens. The miniature hedges that once bordered beds like ornate frames about a picture were banished as unnatural. This was the age of the ha-ha and the uninterrupted view. Landowners did not want garish parrot tulips popping up and ruining the prospect of Capability Brown's new lawn and flooded valley. The tulip fell into the hands of the merchant and artisan class, who, with their natural talent for competition and organization, set up clubs and societies with rules about petal splay and basal blotching and drove the flower into its most perfectly caricatured forms.

When the tulip returned to the great gardens it was as a bedding flower, to be admired en masse in public parks or used to paint great blobs of colour across the pleasure grounds of nineteenth-century financiers. Dutch growers in the flat, sandy fields of the Noordoostpolder had made great leaps forward in the production of tulips, laying down the infrastructure that still today allows my team to order tulips in batches of twenty thousand, to be planted in glades, meadows and dells, where they might either be stumbled upon and admired or ignored completely, flowering only for the blue sky and the bees. Sultan Ahmed III, history's greatest-ever tulip maniac, once bought bulbs by the million and would have scoffed at these quantities, but to me they look impressive coming off the side of a Dutch lorry on the prongs of a forklift truck. We can be so horribly blasé because three dozen Single Lates can be bought for the same price as a pint of beer in my local pub.

Camberwell's most famous tulip grower, the nurseryman Thomas Davey, who grew specialist blooms on a rented plot where the Wyndham Road Post Office now stands, would have been appalled. He had a shop nearby where he once displayed a painting of his favourite tulips as the great figures of the day, George Washington and Napoleon Bonaparte among them, and his 1798 catalogue lists bulbs for up to three hundred pounds. With the day rate for a London labourer having just risen to two shillings, that put them at around the amount a ditch-digger would have earned for three thousand days of solid toil – seven years' work with Sundays off for church and play. A minimum-wage worker today could buy sixty tulips an hour with their pre-tax wages, or seventy if they were on the London living wage.

I suspect most people on Grove Park earn considerably more than seventy tulips an hour. Data from the 2011 census had a median income for the road at fify-five thousand pounds and with inflation taken into account, most households have to be on around half a million tulips a year by now. This begs the question: why are there so few bulb gardens on the Grove? Walking the street on April Fool's Day, I found mature daffodils at No.30, looking very yellow next to a vast, red-flowering Japanese quince (*Chaenomeles japonica*) and a ferociously bright hybrid forsythia (*Forsythia × intermedia*). There were good Darwin-type tulips, probably 'Apeldoorn', not quite in flower, in a turning circle outside No.28. Most of the tree pits had the cheerful dwarf daffodil 'Tête-à-Tête', the hardest-working flower of March, and there were welcome leucojums at No.40, blooming above the green thatch of spent snowdrops. No.43 had a nice bed of cheerful tulips, some out, some still in pear drops of promising bud, and there were patches of crocus in the majority of the small lawns.

By far the most common bulb was the bluebell. As this was London, they were all hybrid bluebells (*Hyacinthoides × massartiana*), a cross between the English bluebell (*Hyacinthoides non-scripta*) and the Spanish bluebell (*Hyacinthoides hispanica*). They were glossy rosettes with flowering spathes just starting to rise at their centre. By late June the plants would be dried splatters on the hard earth with only crispy strands of mucous where their leaves had been. But a dramatic collapse does not mean the plant's work is finished. Some of the roots produced by bluebells are contractile. They grow fat and turgid below the bulb, forcing aside the soil in a cone like that at the underground end of a spring onion. Later these shrink, creating a hole into which other 'pulling' roots drag the bulb. They are retreating from the heat, the dryness and the predators of the surface, burrowing down like razor clams into a sandy beach. It is a growth characteristic shared by many spring bulbs, including daffodils, crocus, hyacinths, muscari and gladioli. The soil beneath a bulb meadow is never still, even in the height of summer. It is seething with invisible pulsations and contractions, with bulbs moving deeper or even sideways, boring a channel along which they will deposit little daughter plants.

Grove Park's best seething meadow is at No.50. On the first day of April, when I lingered by the gate, thankful for the evening light, there were snowdrops in seed, vast amounts of grape hyacinths and clumps of big, bulked-out daffodils, some in flower, some taking the year off, but still welcome for their vigorous spikes of upward energy. There were summer snowflakes, fading woodland crocus (*Crocus tommasinianus*) and there were tulips, glorious lingering clumps of something tall with tantalizing red lines on its blushing buds. Above was a flowering cherry and between everything was front-garden grass of the best kind: slightly tussocky and spangled with primrose and sweet violet (*Viola odorata*).

No.50 is a well-hedged garden and it seemed improper to hover and peer too long. This was a space for the homeowner and that is something to be respected. But the garden still gave abundantly to the street. It was the epicentre of a floral explosion, a seasonally detonated bomb, sending shrapnel two gardens in either direction. These neighbours also had grape hyacinths, primroses and clumps of perfumed violet growing under their hedges and still-bare shrubs. We have a creature that respects boundaries far less than I do to thank for their spread. All three plants are myrmecochorous, meaning they are spread by ants. Their seeds are found by foraging worker ants and carried back to a nest. There they are deposited in front of the larvae who consume the elaiosome, a package of fat and oil that the plant sticks to its seed as an offering to the eyeless white grubs, ever-eating in the darkness beneath the soil. After the larvae have fed, the hard and unpalatable seed is removed and discarded outside on one of the nest's midden heaps, a place where the less digestible bits of insect prey, dead ants, waste and spoil are dumped. Like Persephone, the goddess of spring and germinating grain, the viola (or primrose, or muscari) has returned from the underworld and can work on producing its own offspring, who in their turn will be carried into the deep and pop up again, perhaps a little further down the street.

We humans also have our dark times, but as Solomon got the hang of staying asleep and I was able to cycle home in daylight, they felt far away. The gardeners moved out of the Portakabin and I was able to look at tulips again. I did a lot of smiling, which wasn't very good for the face wrinkles, but I'm going to take a lesson from 'Semper Augustus', the most expensive tulip ever sold, and tell myself that beauty does not come from a petal's freshness, but from the quality of its lines.

# 14

# FLOWERING CHERRY

The last Saturday in February was unexpectedly warm. Sunshine, strong enough to feel, drew people from their houses. On Goose Green they sat on benches, hands on knees, eyes shut, faces tilted to the sky. Groups of friends strolled and laughed on the paths, and beyond the railings small cars with blacked windows and subwoofers cruised by, shaking the ground and making us wonder where they went when it rained. On Peckham Rye circles of picnickers drank and shouted and I navigated by shrub smells; daphne in clean sweet waves, mahonia like citrus on gorse, and Chinese witch hazel (*Hamamelis mollis*) zipping and medical.

London was living again. The joy of things long-missed overflowed. Best of all, the first cherries of spring were blooming on Grove Park. 'If you want a happy ending, that depends, of course, on where you stop your story,' wrote Orson Welles in his last screenplay. Hollywood would have wrapped up the story of our winter on that perfect afternoon; they would have no use for the March-long epilogue, and the final denouement – a week of snow in April – was too ambiguous. No, let the camera pan over the girls on the grass as a Prosecco cork pops, an old lady smiles at the sun, a Golf GTI blasts four-on-the-floor house music and a flurry of petals drifts by. Cue titles, fade to black.

Just a week earlier the temperature was closer to minus ten than zero. On Adys Road, a line of calla lilies (*Zantedeschia aethiopica*) had been beaten black by the frosts and lay halfway to slime on a low wall. At the end of the road an Ethiopian candelabra tree (*Euphorbia abyssinica*) had been tossed in a skip. Several houses had freshly washed paths and everywhere there were paperback books and bits of furniture left out for people to take. Cleaning was in the air, inside houses and out. At the train station I listened to a teenager on the phone. 'I feel really bad, mum,' he kept saying. 'She's going to break up with me, mum. I know she is.' Poor thing, we knew he stood no chance. Blossom was on the air and it was time for change.

The heartbroken boy could perhaps have learned from Grove Park. Up there it is now stable and serene, not ancient, but definitely period. It feels like a road that has reached an equilibrium and is comfortably in love with itself. He would do well to remember that it was once a monstrosity, a scar on the cheek of London that must have felt like it would never heal. Grove Park tore through the cedars of Lebanon (*Cedrus libani*) planted by Dr Lettsom, giants that had been allowed to grow in size and dignity for a century. Their loss was catastrophic and they were mourned. An 1895 article in *The Windsor Magazine* entitled 'The Life of Camberwell' notes: 'The splendid trees that made the loveliness of the park have fallen, to make way for would-be picturesque villas of red-brick.' The author bitterly misses the wooded hilltop the road once was, but still manages to capture the nascent essence of the Grove. Gravitas has given way to a new aura; a bubbling, insistent, suburban energy. The writer admits that, 'There are young trees planted everywhere, and when spring comes you will see more of flowering chestnut, hawthorn, lilac, laburnum, and, later on, of glimmering elder-flower than in ninety-nine out of a hundred towns.' Wounds heal, trees fall, lovers find new lovers. Nothing will bring the cedars back but at least we mourn their loss with the scent of lilac on the air.

The flowering spirit of Grove Park in 1895 remains but few of the species mentioned can now be seen. One flowering chestnut (or horse chestnut, *Aesculus hippocastanum*) grows between the brambles and smashed sofas of No.123. This vast, long-abandoned villa is the biggest single house on the road. It was once a day centre where people on probation could spend mornings in therapy and afternoons learning the violin. Prior to that it had been a convalescent home for injured and infirm police officers. It has been derelict for twenty years.

The Grove has a few hawthorns (*Crataegus*), and lilac (*Syringa vulgaris*) still makes a show where it is allowed. Elderflower (*Sambucus*) survives almost accidentally in the wilder gardens but there is only a single laburnum, an arching multi-stemmed bush on the cusp of treehood that sits in the lawn at 3a. The street is poorer for the near-disappearance of this Victorian favourite – racemes of pineapple-yellow would be heavenly above May's bluebells. However, what is most jarring about *The Windsor Magazine* article is not the species now missing but one that was never mentioned; among the young trees of spring there was no reference to the ornamental cherry (*Prunus*).

For now, the plane is London's emblematic tree. It was not ever thus. In Georgian days this was an elm city. Three centuries from now, London might be a palm tree city, or a Thames-flooded marsh of willow and poplar. It might be a bankrupt, half-paved city of sycamores or a risk-assessed, rubber-stamped city of Callery pears (*Pyrus calleryana*). Most probably though, it will be a land of flowering cherries. Their ascent seems unstoppable. They are already by far the most common tree on London's streets, with the Greater London Authority noting two cherries growing for each plane, yet they were virtually unplanted just a hundred years ago.

The rise of blossom is the great untold story of the twentieth century. We have breeders and enthusiasts to thank. Men and women in Europe, America and Japan, the ornamental cherry's homeland, who formed societies, published bulletins and hunted lost specimens in old gardens. When their experiments and rediscoveries reached nurserymen, the market was flooded with new cultivars; there were chrysanthemum-flowered pinks, weeping forms, upright columns and patio-friendly dwarfs. By 1948 the ornamental cherry was popular enough to earn a lashing from Vita Sackville-West, who described the cultivar 'Kanzan' as 'gaudy' and derided it as 'ubiquitous in the gardens of bungalows, villas and suburbia'.

I agree with Vita, 'Kanzan' is gaudy, but it is also a masterpiece. It is big, pink and double-flowered, and is only everywhere because it is fun. There is a majestic specimen growing from the hedge line at No.53 Grove Park. It has been perfectly pruned over the years, gently shaped to the space, with none of the brutal mid-limb amputations that so often blight the cultivar. 'Kanzan' is perhaps the most hacked-at tree in London. It grows neatly upwards when young and will flower at three years old while still in its showroom pot. It thus inveigles its way into spaces that are too small for its spreading, stout-trunked old age, and is everywhere crudely butchered. As a child, Christopher Lloyd adored its deep rose blossom and copper-tinged young foliage, but in 1994, at the age of seventy-three, he admitted he had outgrown it. This cooling of affections was not something he wished to impose on other gardeners, rather he hoped they would feel its thrill as he once had and ignore the killjoys who point out that 'Kanzan' is considered vulgar in some circles. Those who seek to impose their standards on others are missionaries, he suggested, and missionaries are sometimes 'turned against and murdered for being busybodies'.

Grove Park's cherry show did not open with 'Kanzan', thank the Lord, we needed some warming up. It began slowly with a triangle of *Prunus cerasifera* 'Pissardii', the purple-leaved cherry plum, in the gardens of No.13, No.15 and, across the street, No.50. The dark-leaved trees have a tendency to suck the light from spring and muddy the cloth of summer but on my warm February walk they were at their best, just coming into flower, still months from foliage. Their bark was charcoal and their flowers floated and shone like raindrops in a camera flash. A petal fell on the double yellow lines by the turn-off to Pelham Close and stuck to the rain of the day before. It was a significant moment; for the next twelve weeks there would be cherry blossom in the gutters of Grove Park.

At the end of April the last tree opened. It was undoubtedly the best on the street, filling the large garden of No.35 with blossom so completely that it could have been poured in from a bucket in the sky. Its trunk rose straight and then burst out in a fan of branches, like a cathedral column suddenly hitting its rib vaults. The cultivar was 'Shōgetsu' or, if the Japanese is roughly translated, 'Moonlight on the Pines'. Could a tree have such a name and grow up to be ugly? The flowers budded pink, bloomed white and blushed once more as they faded. They were double-hung in generous pompom clusters from long stalks. Up close it was clear that all practicality had been sacrificed for beauty; a few mangled anthers surrounded a wonky stigma that would never swell with fruit. It was a tree built only to look good.

And built is the word here. This 'Shōgetsu' was assembled from three separate cherries, a surprisingly common practice. The whole thing sat on an underground rootstock, probably *Prunus avium,* the wild cherry. At soil level a straight trunk, the interstem, had been grafted on and the base of the tree did not flare out like the bell of a trumpet, but bulged like an altar candle on a jam doughnut. At the top, high enough for people to pass under, individual branches of the scion had been grafted on. If one September morning we were to take a sharp knife and sever an outer twig, then sink it in sand and perlite until it grew roots of its own, we would have a pure 'Shōgetsu' without the stilt. It would grow almost entirely sideways along the ground, and if it ever made it to flowering, it would do so like a cloud of dry ice on the nightclub floor.

On moving to London from her native Tokyo, the journalist Naoko Abe was struck by the length of the cherry season. She had grown up in a nation where cherry blossom was a 'singular obsession'. Hers was a country where newspapers and television reported on the northward progress of the *sakura zensen*, the blossom front, with friends and colleagues using the bulletins to plan their trip to the park, there to sit among thousands of others, drinking, singing and eating under a pale pink canopy that only the stars and the distant Milky Way could match for beauty. In England, Naoko realized, no such thing would be possible: 'The blooms I encountered here were multicoloured – white, pink, reddish, some even greenish – and the trees blossomed at different times... some of these trees burst into flower, dropped their petals and then another variety would take over, producing a kaleidoscopic cascade effect of blossom that stretched the cherry season to two months.' The revelation set her researching the fate of Japan's once-abundant local cultivars, the trees that would have coloured individual villages before the 'Somei-yoshino' clone became ubiquitous and compressed the spectacle into eight fleeting days. Eventually it led her to Collingwood Ingram, the British gardener and plant collector who became the subject of Abe's remarkable book *'Cherry' Ingram: The Englishman Who Saved Japan's Blossoms*.

The biography contains a masterful passage that sees Collingwood, a one-time ornithologist turned amateur botanist, sitting cross-legged on a mat in the house of the cherry expert Seisaku Funatsu. The pair have spent an afternoon drinking green tea and examining Kōkichi Tsunoi's watercolours of trees in bloom. Eventually Funatsu excuses himself and returns with an ancient scroll. He carefully unrolls the fragile parchment to reveal a painting of an old tree with vast, ice-white flowers. 'This,' says Funatsu, 'is the cherry that my great-grandfather painted more than one hundred and thirty years ago. We used to see it near Kyoto but it seems to be extinct. I can't find it anywhere anymore.' To which Mr Ingram replies, 'This cherry is growing in my garden in Kent!'

Thus 'Tai-haku' (the Great White Cherry) was returned to the Land of the Rising Sun from outside Tunbridge Wells. Ornamental cherry trees have a strong connection with international travel. In January 1910, Tokyo presented Washington with two thousand sapling trees. The accepted narrative is that they were to signify trust, cooperation and love between Japan and the United States after tensions over immigration nearly led to the segregation of Japanese children in California. Charles L Marlatt of the United States Department of Agriculture did not care for international relations. He inspected the dormant saplings and reported that they had gall of the crown, gall of the root and scale (two types). Their wood contained a boring beetle that was possibly new to science and six other insects classed as dangerous. Marlatt recommended they be incinerated and President William Howard Taft had no choice but to agree. On the 28th of January the symbolic olive branches lay in burning pyres across the Washington Monument.

This is not the only time a gift of trees has failed. On 7th May 1977 *The New York Times* reported on President Jimmy Carter's visit to Newcastle, or as they put it, 'a grimy corner of industrial Britain.' The Lord Mayor told the president, 'You have now become Geordie.' Carter turned to the ten thousand spectators and shouted 'Haway the lads!' The next day the President visited the village of Washington, ancestral home of George Washington, and 'at the small village green, overlooked by two pubs and an ancient church with weathered, tilting gravestones, Mr Carter ceremonially planted a small tulip poplar tree.'

A month later *The Washington Post* ran an article headlined: 'Tree Carter Planted in England Dies.' State Department officer Midge Burke briefed the paper, adopting the manner of a doctor with bad news: 'It could not adjust to the change in climate...they had three surgeons look at it last week. It was still wilted. It's not going to survive.' I believe that this is an example of a senior official lying on record. A 1984 interview with the United States Chief of Protocol reveals that it was not spring in the Northeast that killed the tree – along with several back-up plants, it froze in the plane's cargo hold and was dead even as the band played 'Blaydon Races' and Carter waved his ceremonial shovel. 'Apparently, they didn't look so bad,' said the spokesman. 'So they went ahead with the symbolic planting.'

To return to 1910 and the burning saplings, Emperor Meiji took the potential insult well. A second shipment was arranged, this time of six thousand cherries, three thousand and twenty of which were planted around the Tidal Basin in West Potomac Park. Today millions visit Washington DC to see the Japanese cherry trees in flower.

The National Trust is proposing a Big British Blossom Watch to bring our divided nation together, like Washington and Tokyo. It won't match the *hanami* picnics of Japan – we lack the monoculture. Instead the Trust offers a social media hashtag and a 'blossom activity pack' for people to download. The idea is laudable; to connect people with the natural world. But connecting people who are not ready is hard. I spent cherry season attempting to interest Solomon in the blooms of Grove Park – those pink clouds of April, and the petal showers of May. We made detours from nursery and I said, 'Look, cherry, cherry, *look*!' Once he pointed up with excitement, but of course he was looking beyond the boughs at an aeroplane on its way to Heathrow.

I worry about my son's connection with nature. In those fuzzy half-forgotten weeks when he was a newborn, I read Coleridge's hopeful poem *Frost at Midnight* for his own infant son, Hartley. The lines:

...For I was rear'd
In the great city, pent 'mid cloisters dim,
And saw nought lovely but the sky and stars.
But thou, my babe! shalt wander, like a breeze
By lakes and sandy shores...'

They almost set me crying. I was raised in beauty and yet I was keeping Sol, my most precious thing, pent in the great city. My guilt was added to over the next eighteen months when everyone we knew with children began to drift away from London. People we met in our pre-birth parenting classes, the nice young strangers with whom we learned about pelvic trauma, started to leave for Surrey and Buckinghamshire. Other friends went to Pembrokeshire. My brother sailed his canal boat and his own toddler out of the East End and into a nature reserve miles north of the M25.

I try to remind myself that Coleridge's bond with the heavens might have been formed because of his smoke-shrouded childhood, not despite it. As a boy he had only the sky and the stars, but he *saw* those stars, and he loved them. I know people raised by actual sandy shores who describe their childhood as 'boring' and 'a bit crap'. I was brought up at the foot of the Hampshire Hangers, in the heart of Gilbert White country, but at my school no one noticed the beech unfurling. The wooded hills were a lumpy backdrop to more urgent teenage dramas.

If Solomon is to be nourished by beauty, as I am now, he will find it where he needs to. It is waiting for him up in the Lake District, but it is also in the garden of No.35. If, by some chance, he chooses not to spend his youth like Coleridge, marvelling at the play of light on a limpid pool, or even like Christopher Lloyd, thrilling at the vivid flush of a 'Kanzan' cherry, and somehow ends up with more usual adolescent interests, then well, London is great for those too. He can buy a Golf GTI and a sound system, and when he first gets his heart broken, I'll take him up to Grove Park and tell him that terrible changes don't stay terrible forever.

# 15

# MAGNOLIA

Edith Wharton was not drawn to the poor and the ordinary. This was a woman who dined with Henry James at the Villa Medici, who wrote novels in bed, completing each page and throwing it off the side for her secretary to find and type out. For decades she froze the high society of America and Europe on her pages, then froze them again, in person, at their parties. However, in her early short story *Mrs Manstey's View*, she takes an enjoyable detour into a more ordinary reality.

Mrs Manstey rents a room in a shabby New York brownstone. All day she sits at the window, her mind entirely on the view. She is almost interested in the people she sees (noisy slatterns, she surmises), but it is the glimpsed gardens that attract her. They are disordered wastes mostly, but there is a magnolia in the next lot, and a wisteria that flowers each May.

The widow half-listens to her infrequent visitors and wishes they would leave. After seventeen years with her eyes on their branches and blossom, she finds it hard to tear herself from the plants. They have 'surrounded and shaped her life as the sea does a lonely island'. Her landlady pops up and Mrs Manstey daringly breaks with convention and talks about her true love. 'The magnolia is out earlier than usual this year, Mrs Sampson,' she ventures. The reply she receives could not be more shocking. 'Is it, indeed?' says Mrs Sampson. 'I didn't know there was a magnolia there.'

The story ends in arson and death, but on the way it is a precise observation on subjective experience. If just one thing matters, then it matters a lot. Mrs Manstey's life has been boiled down to almost nothing but her passions have not cooked off, they have just been concentrated. The landlady's ignorance of the flowering magnolia is a sign of a world gone wrong. Mrs Manstey must sharpen her metaphorical sword and be prepared to fight for what she loves, and fight alone. It's a good story but I wish Wharton hadn't chosen magnolia as the plant of revelation. It's unrealistic and breaks the illusion. If a magnolia is in flower then *everyone* knows it's in flower.

Magnolias are thermogenic and their blooms produce real cellular heat. This is thought be a reward for pollinating beetles and an encouragement for them to linger. Our traditional garden magnolias, the ones foregrounding those Cookham paintings by Stanley Spencer, come from the forests of East Asia where spring can be cold and long. What a boon the candle of warmth must be for Zhejiang Province sap beetles, newly emerged in early March with snow still on the hills. Mrs Manstey herself could not appreciate the petals more.

A secondary effect of magnolia's metabolic warming is an amplification of the tree's scent, a sweet, lemony tang, dominated by linalool, the terpene alcohol found in tangerine peel and lavender flowers. The temperature peaks when the flower is in its female phase. It then dips and spikes again when the bloom enters its subsequent male stage. Female-then-male maturation lessens the chance of self-pollination. The stigma are receptive before the petals have even opened. They are waiting for pollen-strewn beetles to force their way into the bud after feeding in another tree. By the time the flower is fully open and producing male gametophytes, its own ovaries have become inaccessible. Beetles remain in the cooling bloom, consuming the calorie-rich pollen, and then follow the lavender and tangerine smells to the next warm, female-phase tree. It is an elegant and simple solution, befitting magnolia's status as the premier 'primitive' plant.

Perhaps this pre-flowering fertility is why magnolias are unusually attractive in the week before they open. At No.4 Grove Park there are two spreading trees, both hybrid *soulangeana* cultivars. From St David's Day, on the first of March, cream and magenta candles stood on their bare wood like chicory hearts, each aligned to the sky no matter the angle of the branch below. They stopped people on the pavement and made them point. Many buds are beautiful. There is a clematis growing behind the bike stands on Warwick Square in central London that stuns me every spring. It looks as if a champagne meteor has fizzed along the railings, leaving sprigs of bright, rosé-tinged bubbles in its wake. But the elation it provokes is anticipatory, it comes with knowing the ironwork will soon be buried in cruciform flowers. A budding magnolia does not need the promise of a finale, it is perfect in that moment alone. The clematis is dawn on a wedding day, made beautiful by what is to come, the magnolia is sunrise itself. And all because it favours beetles over bees.

Had the magnolia evolved in a time of bees it might have shaped itself to make better use of them. It would not have such robust and architectural flowers. Bees are remarkable pollinators and there is no need to trap them in a thick-walled floral cavern to ensure the job gets done. They are the posited answer to Charles Darwin's famous 'abominable mystery' of why higher plants appear in the fossil record so suddenly at the end of the Cretaceous period and diversify so incredibly quickly. The flying bee, as an unparalleled distributer of DNA, kicked off a bidding war between angiosperms – more petals, more nectar and more specialized means of its delivery. Come to me, says one plant, my tube is long and my juice is sweet, perfect for that extended tongue you seem to be developing; you'll recognize me by my blue petals, let's co-evolve. Another hawks good, dense calories at the stem with the red sepals and promises to bloom in a conveniently simultaneous rush, all across the forest and savannah. Honey bees like to feed on one flower at a time; they will sup on heather until the heather is finished and then move on to gorse. This is why we can produce monofloral honeys like chestnut and manuka from bees that have two square miles of diverse forage.

A bee that will fly over all distractions to spread pollen between members of a single species is a remarkable tool in the survival of the fittest. But it was not available to the magnolias when they developed their beetle-baiting aroma and their waxy petals. They sit within the family Magnoliaceae in an ancient order that appeared ninety-six million years ago and has changed little since. Magnoliales debuted in the Cenomanian Age when Earth's seas were at their highest and a marine reptile floating above one-day-to-be-London could swing its bus-length neck south and swim over the coral reef we call France (passing fern-covered islands that would become the Alps) into the Indian Ocean. The beetles and the magnolias were alone together for a further thirty million years before dinosaurs went extinct and the bees appeared, by which time our plant was well set in its ways.

In Grove Park, now dried out and 30 yards above sea level, the magnolia at No.102 comes out first. It faces south, on the hot side of the street, with a brick wall at its back and the black road at its feet. Opposite, in the garden of north-facing No.70, an identical plant follows it into flower a few days later. I wonder if beetles pass between them, commuting south from male phase to female over the parked BMWs and the little white Mazda. It would be a journey unknown in nature before the last two centuries. These plants are *Magnolia* × *soulangeana*, a hybrid created in the 1820s by Etienne Soulange-Bodin, a French cavalry officer recently returned from the Napoleonic wars. He took pollen from the deep purple mulan magnolia (*Magnolia liliiflora*), deposited it on the stigma of the pure white yulan magnolia (*Magnolia denudata*), and from the seed raised a beautiful Frankenstein's monster, fresh born from ancient parts. His plant was a smash, the entire stock bought out by hungry nurserymen who saw profit in its parts, its father's quickness to flower, its mother's stature and elegance, and its flowers – a couldn't-have-designed-it-better gradient of paternal pink fading into maternal white.

This is the magnolia we know. Stanley Spencer's magnolia. The magnolia our grandparents planted and left in their front gardens for us to enjoy. They survive better than any other tree, because what kind of psychopath would cut down a mature magnolia? There were peaks of planting in the 1930s and the 1950s, and London swims in seventy- and ninety-year-old specimens. These old trees fit their front gardens perfectly. These are trees coded for the forest glade. They do not try to pierce an imaginary canopy or lean away from the shadow of the house. Their forbears lived in the shade of Daurian birch and Mongolian oak and they grow symmetrically, even when the light is poor.

The two magnolias at No.4 spread as wide as they are tall. Money can't purchase trees like these. They are bought in instalments, summer by summer, bud-break to leaf-drop, paid for in time itself. When I worked for the oligarch, our brief was absurd: 'Build the best garden in London. Better than the Queen's.' This order was delivered by a trusted hanger-on, a man with a budget matched only by his paranoia. He once appeared with a printout of our projected outgoings and shouted, 'You say you want to buy trees? But we have trees! Look! Tree, tree, tree!' He pointed three times at different parts of an overgrown thuja hedge, left staked and half-strangled by previous owners. We explained that these were not good trees and that they would never have been allowed to grow at Buckingham Palace. The spend was eventually signed off and the oligarch's assistant retreated, telling us to buy the best trees in England, he would know if we hadn't.

But, of course, we didn't buy the best trees in England. There was no way we could. The best trees in England are not for sale. They are wedded to the place they have grown. Within a half mile of that North London mansion there were a thousand trees better than all the stock advertised in the nurseries of Kent, Italy and Holland. Those fragile, aged things had crowns wider than the slow lane of the M20 from Dover. They wouldn't tessellate, sardine-like, on the back of an articulated lorry, as trussed up *Liquidambar styraciflua* 'Slender Silhouette' would. The hundreds of thousands of pounds spent on plants for the oligarch's garden got him nothing approaching the quality of the trees at No.4. If you want something as magnificent as the Grove Park magnolias, you do what the rest of us do: you plant it and bloody well wait. In a world where private jets were chartered to keep hairdressers in the right city, it was nice to know that even billions cannot buy everything.

Mrs Loftie, a Victorian writer on household design and management, once declared, 'Ignorance and want of taste in those who have money to spend must always have a fatal effect upon everything produced. Rich people...can only judge of the merits of their pleasure-ground by the length of the bills.' She was right. The best garden in London is subjective, the most expensive is not. It became clear that to keep things sweet with the oligarch's entourage his garden should shout VIP. The lawn needn't appear inviting – there would be no picnics; it needed to look ready to accept a helicopter at any moment, along with all the high heels, designer loafers and ex-army steel toecaps it might disgorge. All the windowboxes of the Dorchester and the Ritz emptied around a golf course was the style to hit.

On the last Saturday in March, I toured the Grove magnolias in strong sunshine. The shredded-tissue spume of the *Magnolia stellata* at No.17 was fun, and I appreciated the Council's imagination in putting two *Magnolia liliiflora* out on the pavement; my street is under the same local authority and all we get is Callery pear (*Pyrus calleryana*). At No.4 the saucer magnolias flowered blowsily. No longer elegant candelabras, they were in full, male-stage display, petals flapping, each gothic bud unfurled into exuberant rococo nonsense. A man with a brown ponytail and a leather satchel stopped underneath and bent backwards to take a picture. He stayed that way for a long time, in quarter limbo, his phone held in front of his face as though he were working up to swallow it. The image he took is probably spectacular, perfect spring-blue sky seen through a flamingo-storm of pink and white. Let's hope it inspires him to plant a tree of his own. I did not spend quite as long at No.4, though I did get some photos of my own. Instead, I carried on up the road and round the corner to No.52, home to the moodiest tree on Grove Park.

George Washington had a horse called Magnolia. Many assume it was the white stallion in those portraits by Stuart, Sully and Trumbull, the one posing with its tail raised, ready to defecate over the city of Charleston. But no, that's Blueskin. Magnolia was a reddish-chestnut Arabian. As befits the 'Father of his Country', Washington named his horse for the rust- and copper-toned underleaf of a true American icon, the evergreen *Magnolia grandiflora*. If his colour-naming convention had stuck, anyone who 'went with the safe choice' and painted their hallway magnolia would be returning each day to a room as brown as old oil drums.

At the turn of 1784, Washington had spent just eighteen days in eight-and-a-half years of war at his plantation. With the British surrender he resigned his commission, commended his country 'to the protection of Almighty God' and went home to grow trees. He was not very good at it. In the spring of 1785 his diary records:

Most of my transplanted trees have a sickly look.
The small Pines in the Wildernesses are entirely dead...
Almost the whole of the Holly are dead. Many of the Ivy,
wch. before looked healthy & well seem to be declining.
Few of the Crab Tree had put forth leaves. Not a single
Ash tree has unfolded its buds...The lime trees, which had
some appearance of Budding when I went away, are now
withering and the Horsechesnut & Tree box from Colo.
Harry Lee's discover little signs of shooting. The Hemlock
is almost entirely dead, & bereft of their leaves and so are
the live Oak. In short half the Trees in the Shrubberies,
& many in the Walks, are dead.

But he did not give up. On the 2nd of May 1786, he writes, 'Planted 140 Seed sent me by Colo. Wm. Washington and said by him to be the Seed of the large Magnolio or Laurel of Carolina.' This is *Magnolia grandiflora*. The year after he set them in the ground he left Mount Vernon for Philadelphia and the Constitutional Convention, and three years later became the first President of the new United States. Had I met him in the summer of 1786 I might have advised him to take it easy, don't go up to Philadelphia; winning a war and planting even a single *Magnolia grandiflora* is enough legacy for any man. One only needs to visit the garden of 52 Grove Park to know that.

On my late March walk the evergreen tree was in perfect contrast to the cherry clouds and daffodil trumpets blazing elsewhere. Its trunk was closer to the fence than the house, and while its branches snaked down to the ground on three sides, they had been cut back from the pavement, giving passersby the impression that it was lifting its skirts and inviting them into the dark world beneath. It was fragrant there. An underplanting of sweet olive (*Osmanthus* × *burkwoodii*), white-flowering, even in the gloom, pumped out a smell like apricot violets. A New Zealand flax (*Phormium tenax*) had been swallowed and sulkily sprawled next to a blue-flowering periwinkle and in front of a stand of low laurustine (*Viburnum tinus*). The rest of the clearing was covered in finely lobed ornamental ivy, black-green where it lay on the floor, fresh shooting as it licked the tree's trunk. This was such an obviously sunless place that there had been no half-successful attempt to grow grass, no thin blades rising from a mud sea. There I was treated to real understorey planting.

The hero or heroine responsible for 52's *grandiflora* is probably dead like George Washington. I say this because the tree is strikingly mature, at least fifty years old, perhaps climbing towards a century, and specimen-tree planting is a middle-aged game. It is hard to tell the precise age of these slow-growing evergreens. I have visited one of Europe's oldest *Magnolia grandiflora*, planted at the Orto Botanico di Padova in the same year Washington set his seeds. Apart from buttress roots that splayed squid-like over the stones, it did not look ancient. It had been well cared for. If one of the university *giardinieri* had accidentally broken its leading shoot in the 1780s, or botched its pruning in the 1810s, it would have developed more of the crags and eccentricities we associate with extreme age. It would then be multi-stemmed and fused. There would be bits of redundant growth that had been allowed to rot. It might well be hollow and full of owls. But no traumatic blow occurred and it has grown on a single trunk up to its natural height and slowly thickened. The tree at No.52 was doing largely the same.

There were some scars high up and facing the road, perhaps from work on a telephone line, but they would need decades of fungal decay before they could serve as roosts for Grove Park's noctule bats. I hope they deepen – the *grandiflora* deserves bats. In the swamps of South Carolina it would be festooned in Spanish moss (*Tillandsia usneoides*), the hanging, cobweb plant that carries the 'southern gothic' look in films about murder on the bayou. The sight of a foot-wide, lemon-scented magnolia flower opening through a curtain of undead green is surely on every plant-watcher's bucket list, but a bat flitting into the summer dusk from a cavern in a tree as old as the dinosaurs would be a good Camberwell substitute. Or so I thought to myself as I bundled off, beetle-like, towards the next of the Grove's priceless trees.

# 16

## IRIS

In early May the swallows returned. Not that I saw any – they haven't bred in Camberwell since 1945 – but it was nice to know they were back and dancing again over some distant green. They made me think of Gilbert White and how he spent all that time with Timothy, his tortoise, and thus reasoned his way out of accepting trans-continental migration. The logic went: in winter's mild spells Timothy briefly wakes; I have seen swallows flying on warm afternoons in December; Hampshire is too far from Africa to make the journey for one warm day, *ergo,* swallows, like tortoises, hibernate in holes in the ground and emerge when the weather is pleasant.

In Gilbert's time the birds would certainly have flown over Grove Park. He wrote that they dipped and cornered in all the wide, new parts of the capital, avoiding only the city centre. They are a sad loss to us. One hundred and twenty years before Gilbert's *The Natural History of Selborne* was published, we Londoners were intimately connected to the swallow. We were skin-close. By which I mean we used to boil up swallows and rub them on our arms and legs.

In the *Pharmacopoeia Londinensis* of the Royal College of Physicians, put into English by Nicholas Culpeper in 1649 as *A Physicall Directory, or a Translation of the London Dispensatory*, there is a recipe for making Oyl of Swallows. It calls for sixteen swallows, whole and alive, chamomile, bay, pennyroyal, dill, rosemary and sage, over which should be poured four pounds of common oil (though butter will do if you can't get it), and a pound of Spanish wine. All to be cooked into an ointment and saved for rubbing on bruises and sprains.

If we accept this as magic, not medicine, it is easy to see how the swallow is gifted with powers of renewal and healing. They arrive, from who knows where, when the earth is at its most spring-like and perfect, and skip over a land that is suddenly alive, wreathed with flies, gnats and tiny drifting spiders. If I were feeling beat-up and old, if a sprained ankle were tying me to the ground with a heavy rope of pain, I would want nothing more than to be as weightless as the swallow, to skim over the

Thames with my mouth held wide. To be as young as the new year. I'd ask my doctor for the Oyl and make him go light on the chamomile.

The swallows reached England in significant numbers on the first warm days after a cold April. Had the birds broken with their tradition and come back to South London, they would have found it as green and soft as an aphid belly. We all delighted in the lushness. Several times that week I came back with my shoulders damp. I had been treading habitual paths, stepping one side of the lamppost, avoiding the people at the bus stop by dodging round the bin, but the gaps I was aiming for had shrunk as the lime trees and the beech hedges unfurled delicate new leaves that wetted me with the raindrops of the night before. Everything was fresh. Even the ivy's new growth was tender and almost translucent, the colour of pea purée. The council workers had fallen behind on their spraying, thank God, and the seams of the pavements were picked out in grass and weeds, as though the world was an emerald balloon on which Southwark had been painted and it was now cracking as it expanded. Best of all, on the Grove the bearded irises were out.

The upward energy of the iris is staggering. I know that to us chroniclers of spring (and it's not only me; on the 2nd of May, a poster was up at the end of Grove Park that said,

'Lost: blue drawstring rucksack containing a leaf notebook and some green apples' – a poet's day bag if there ever was one), all growth is a miracle, but most plants make being alive look harder. Smooth and steely, the iris leaves rise from nowhere. Where was it all stored? The answer is in the rhizomes, swollen beige batteries that lie half out of the soil. We are watching last year's light be recycled.

I took a day off work in the wet days at the end of spring. Kat and I dropped Solomon at nursery and walked along the Grove, travelling east into the rising sun, with Camberwell behind us and Peckham ahead. In the tree pit outside No.59, a tall bearded iris (*Iris germanica*) sprang from a jumble of campanula and soft Turkish sage (*Phlomis russeliana*). Where its leaves escaped the shadow of the plane tree, they glowed in the slanting light. Each was the shape of a Roman gladius – that fat sword designed to be thrust from one man's hip to another man's stomach. They looked strong and pleasantly vicious. Christopher Lloyd believed it essential to have spiked plants amid the soft domes of an English garden. He thought they gave a lift, 'like the first glass of Champagne on a Sunday morning'. I wholeheartedly agree.

I proposed that No.83 had the best irises on the Grove and Kat agreed. On the left-hand side of the small shallow garden were Dutch irises (*Iris* × *hollandica*), which grow from bulbs, not tubers. They flowered above the last petals of the bluebells and the first flowers of French lavender (*Lavandula stoechas*). Two shades of blue were out already, with a yellow still in bud. As in every one of the three hundred or so species in the genus, the flowers had three petals. These were held upright, almost meeting above the plant's head, like a ballerina with arms *en haut*. Below were three sepals, just as beautiful but bigger, starting in a tube and flaring out into a big drooping lip like the lolling tongue of a paint-eating labrador. In iris-breeding circles they do away with the terms petal and sepal, and refer to the upward pointing bits as 'standards' and the downward flaps as 'falls'.

Towards the house there were bigger flowers. A group of classic bearded irises, violet on the standards, indigo on the falls, with a caterpillar of bright yellow hairs at their haft, the 'beard' from which this group takes its name. The garden's right-hand corner bore flowers that were taller and showier still with ruffled purple falls and standards the colour of stewed rhubarb. I suspect they were the old cultivar 'Bruno'. Their effect was magically old-fashioned, with the shape and colour of a dowager Victorian in velvet skirts and a frilled blouse. Wonderful to look at, but not if you are into silhouettes, which could be considered a pity, as the iris has the most recognizable and loveliest silhouette of any flower. The wild rose has a pretty bloom, but on outline alone it could be any of a thousand five-petalled things from the family Rosaceae. A sunflower and a daisy are identical in cut-out. Even wisteria looks like laburnum, which resembles robinia. Only the iris is unique – it is the ancient fleur-de-lis of the French kings.

Down the hill from 83, Kat and I continued our iris walk and reached the glorious garden at No. 24. We were kept from the lawn and the pots of Darjeeling banana (*Musa sikkimensis*) by sixty-five railings, each topped with a fleur-de-lis. In these heraldic symbols, the iris standards merge to form the spike and their falls become the scrolls. The iron petals were hardly distinguishable, they had merged until the whole flower looked like the spades from a deck of cards. By December the other irises on the Grove will all be gone. They are destined to retreat into their roots, taking their sugars with them. The swallows will go back to Africa, and the *germanica* by 59, with its leaves like a legionary's sword, will fall in on itself, raggedly diminishing until it is a little brown bobble on the plane tree's roots. The Dutch irises at 83 will suck back into the soil and the grand old lady in rhubarb and bat-wings will be cut down with secateurs into a little fan, before shrivelling away as the leaves rush down to bury her. Then all that remains will be the flowers of black metal.

We bring our own meanings to the plants. Louise Glück won the Pulitzer Prize for her poetry collection *The Wild Iris*. It is a staggering work in which a gardener-poet debates existence and the everlasting with God, with breakaway dialogues between the grower and her plants. Wordsworth once wrote: 'To me the meanest flower that blows can give / Thoughts that do often lie too deep for tears.' Glück takes these thoughts and scalpels them into the page. A white rose, knowing it cannot survive more than a summer, looks up in the shredding dark and asks the gardener, 'Explain my life to me, you who make no sign though I call out to you in the night.' Before concluding, 'You are not the light I called to / but the darkness behind it.' In Glück's garden, man, God and Nature have reached an uncomprehending impasse. But there is one flower that speaks of hope. It is the wild iris of the title. 'At the end of my suffering there was a door,' it says. 'Hear me out: that which you call death I remember…it is terrible to survive as consciousness buried in the dark earth.' But the flower has returned from cold oblivion, and from the centre of its life comes 'a great fountain, deep blue / shadows on azure seawater'.

The iris speaks with Eurydice, reminding us that it is as much a plant of the underworld as of the sunny plain. Ignore the banners of Clovis I and Louis VII, for most of human history it has been the root of the bearded iris that carried its worth. Along with the Oyl of Swallows in the *Pharmacopoeia Londinensis*, just before Oyl of Earthworms (take half a pound of earthworms, two pounds of olive oil and eight ounces of wine, etc.), there is a recipe for Oyl of Orris, made from the root of the 'orris florentine'. This is the legendary white iris of Florence, now classified as a variant of *Iris germanica* (*Iris germanica* var. *florentina*). It grew wild on the walls of that Tuscan city and it now grows on Grove Park, the last plants, bar the buddleja, we passed leaving Camberwell.

They sat on a wild patch that had been half-gardened, sharing their space with nettles (*Urtica dioica*), goose grass (*Galium aparine*) and green alkanet (*Pentaglottis sempervirens*) that had crawled under the weld-mesh fence from the railway embankment beyond. The plants were well established and probably three or four years old. Whoever set down the rhizomes had, knowingly or otherwise, connected us to the ancients. Pliny the Elder writes of the iris root, recommending it for unguents and headaches and warning that, 'not only when dried, but also when in the ground, it is very easily subject to worms'. Which can be read as sensible advice not to plant it in waterlogged conditions. He also recommended that those gathering orris should be chaste, which seems less sound. Aretaeus of Cappadocia, writing in the 2nd century CE, recommended coating a feather in extract of iris root and introducing it to the throat of a child suffering epilepsy. Theophrastus, a student of Plato's, a companion to Aristotle and a man considered the father of botany, thought the iris root perfume was at its best three years after collection, but he knew of a perfumer who had a cache of twenty-year-old Egyptian rhizomes, and who swore they were in good condition, better even than his freshly ground stock. Plutarch agreed. In the section of his *Moralia* considering 'Whether an Old Man Should Engage in Public Affairs', he lauded the aged, saying that they were 'free from ostentation and desire for popularity, and, therefore, just as they say that the iris, when it has grown old and has blown off its fetid and foul smell, acquires a more fragrant odour, so no opinion or counsel of old men is turbulent, but they are all weighty and composed'. Students of recent history might disagree, but that old iris smells nice is not in doubt.

Its use continues in modern times. A Victorian correspondent to *The Field* recommended a half-inch piece be given to constipated peregrine falcons and another noted that in Austria and Germany it was dyed bright colours and thrown on the fire to perfume a room. He added that large quantities of the raw root were chewed by waiters and servants on the continent, who deployed it to hide the stink of garlic and tobacco on their breath. Today, powdered orris root is used as a fragrant fixative in potpourri and as a botanical in Beefeater gin, the makers of which occasionally find the price driven up when orris-heavy perfumes such as Chanel No.19 cycle into fashion. The pure orris fragrance is of a damp rag dipped in violet essence and buried in the best mushroom compost: floral but dirty. And Theophrastus was right, it is better when well aged.

We do not powder our *Iris germanica* roots at work, but we do heed Pliny and keep them dry. It is a myth that the rhizomes need to be planted only half-submerged, like a floating duck. They do not need sunlight to bake and will flower happily under half an inch of soil. But horticultural canards exist for a reason. Telling gardeners that the top of the root must always be on display stops us getting confused and planting them like bulbs – six inches down in the dark, where any emerging leaves will fold up against the soil and rot. I use *Iris germanica* in hot narrow spaces where energetic uplift is required and I use its cousin, the native yellow flag iris (*Iris pseudacorus*) everywhere else.

The yellow flag is an explosive flower. Its four-inch blooms open in under a second, a magnificent sight if one has an afternoon to waste, unblinking, in the borders. This is not a unique characteristic in the floral kingdom. *Cornus canadensis* flowers unfurl in half a millisecond, but they have a trigger (the attentions of a bee) and a definite aim (to drive pollen into the insect's hair at twenty-four thousand metres per second). African mistletoes in the family Loranthaceae use the same tactic, waiting for the beak of a nectar-drinking sunbird to probe the seams in its petals and then bursting in a cloud of microgametophytes. The yellow iris has no such aim. In bud its falls are wrapped tightly round each other, three times each, all anticlockwise; nine layers of petal twisting into a point. Pressure begins to build at the base of the unopened flower, putting more and more strain on the knot at the tip until the whole thing unties and the falls and standards spring out into their finished form.

*Iris pseudacorus* is not prone to rot and grows happily almost submerged on the edge of water courses. At work we dot it through a large, wet, tropical border as flutes of champagne in a sea of rum punch. It brings some upright zing to the spreading leaves of ligularia, banana, ferns and candelabra primroses. Our only complaint is that the flowers are at their best for just twenty-four hours each, breaking suddenly yellow like a dropped egg and fading by teatime the next day. In fact, most irises put on a surprisingly short show, given their outsized blooms. A simple *Iris germanica* expends huge effort on each bud, only to get briskly fertilized and retract into itself, as though a suction pump had been switched on deep in the rhizome. A more complicated bloom such as the bicolour 'Bruno' at No.83 Grove Park cannot fold and the old petals plaster round the stem like an umbrella with a broken catch. It has been suggested that a short and obvious window of opportunity stops bees wasting their time on dried-up flowers and ensures they visit only the blooms where the pollen is freshest.

Some irises in the Oncocyclus Group can maintain their show for longer, with individual standards and falls held aloft for almost a week. It is no coincidence that they also show the best scarlet tones in the genus. The compound eyes of a bee are less able than ours to pick up the long waves of electromagnetic radiation we perceive as red (this is why so many true red flowers are hummingbird-pollinated). An iris flower's sole purpose is to attract insects and it makes no evolutionary sense to camouflage its flowers, unless it is disguising them as something attractive. Red-petalled irises such as the exceptionally large-flowered and striking *Iris atropurpurea* are not offering a meal, they are giving a bed for the night. A study of the plant growing wild on the Israeli coastal plain found that after dusk a high proportion of flowers contained sleeping male bees, all of them members of a solitary species in the Eucerini tribe. These irises are shelter mimics. The flowers, which seem so achingly beautiful to us, are trying their best to look like nothing more than a rock with a hole in it.

Human perspectives change, sometimes remarkably quickly. There are periods when our wavelengths seem to expand and we see colour and detail where before there were only outlines in the blackness. In the span of two lives we went from the *Pharmacopoeia Londinensis* and its recipe for 'The Way to Burn Swallows' – 'Sprinkle them with a little salt, and burn them in an earthen vessel well glazed, and keep the Ashes for your use. After the same manner are burnt Hedgehogs, Toads, and Frogs, but without salt'– to Gilbert White's meticulous records and correspondence on when the first returning birds were seen, and whether they might hibernate en masse in the white cliffs of Sussex or migrate to Senegal. And yet some things are universal. In 1967 archaeologists discovered a buried bronze-age town on Santorini. Since the middle of the 2nd century CE it had lain under thick ash from the catastrophic volcanic eruption that blew a hole in the island back when it was still called Thera. For three-and-a-half thousand years the frescoes inside every building were interred, hidden from light, air and sight, until, like Glück's azure flower, they returned from oblivion. Among the joyous paintings are a pair of swallows kissing above wild plants, and a woman with an unmistakable jewelled flower in her hair. It is the iris-inspired fleur-de-lis.

# 17

# LONDON PRIDE

At twenty minutes past six on the 28th of October 1944 a V2 rocket blew up over Grove Park. Two minutes earlier it had been above the North Sea, as long as an eighteen-wheel truck and moving faster than the speed of sound. An American pilot, overtaken by one of the missiles in the dark, recalled: 'It resembled a meteor, streaming red sparks and whizzing past us as though the aircraft were motionless.'

If you caught the roar of a V2, it had already gone by. 'I heard nothing and I saw nothing coming,' a survivor reported. 'I saw houses opposite rise in the air and there was the most terrible noise and explosion.' When the TNT and ammonium nitrate lit up Camberwell, the British government had not yet acknowledged the existence of German supersonic rockets. They feared demoralization. People learning they had lived through five years of war to come under attack from unmanned and unstoppable ballistic weapons, each weighing thirteen tons and arrowing down from the edge of space, might well just give up and lie down.

Throughout the war the morale of the city was of concern. Noël Coward did his bit by writing war tunes. He despaired of the dirge-like patriotic songs rolled out in the Blitz and in 1941 he wrote to Jack Wilson to say:

> [People] should take a lighter view than Miss Durbin did when she sang 'There'll Always Be an England' with tears rolling down her face as though she were bitterly depressed at the thought. I have written one of the best songs of my life called 'London Pride'.

For Noël, London pride (*Saxifraga × urbium*) becomes an emblem of the city's fortitude under fire. In his cheerful song it is the floral companion to the cockney sparrow, the yawning policeman and the rain on a Park Lane pavement. But even in our less emotionally heightened times the plant's draw is clear. It lives year-round as a carpet of low, evergreen rosettes. In May and June an elegant panicle rises from the heart of each whorl, dusting the air between knee height and mid-shin with tiny white and pink flowers. A single rosette would hold its own on any gravel bench, but we can have it by the thousands, in almost any bed we choose and in such profusion that the ground seems to fizz. It spreads in sun or shade, moving out on creeping stolons and rooting as it goes. Unlike some space-filling plants, which scribble off in random directions, leaving bare patches and gaps behind the lines, London pride meticulously covers every inch available before moving on. It does not surrender ground it has already taken and its clumps do not die out in the middle as other carpeting rock plants do.

On Grove Park it would love anywhere bergenias are grown: the gloomy spaces under high-stepping shrubs, the awkward shadow where the north side of a fence meets the ground. But it can also be dragged into prime positions – as filler for the holes where herbaceous perennials meet the garden path. In full sun the leaves of the rosette stand almost straight up, showing just their notched top edge. In the shade they grow longer and more prostrate, each one the shape of those little sample spoons the *gelato* man hands out when you've forgotten what *stracciatella* tastes like. The plant is creating a wider, flatter circle, so as not to lose any of the available light. It means that in sunny situations London pride will always have more flowers, as more, tighter rosettes are crammed into each square foot, but in gloom it will range wider and hide more soil.

I adore *Saxifraga × urbium* for the way it smudges hard landscaping, rushing to the edge of paths and casting itself a couple of inches onto the slabs. It softens a design without obscuring it. Famously, London pride was used as a ribbon to front Victorian dahlia and gladioli beds, and it retains the musty scent of those days. Surely it is due to be shaken out and repurposed. It would be staggeringly effective in a futurist foliage garden, where it could green the gaps between rectangles of poured concrete and black water. Ultra-modernity has not reached Grove Park, and here it grows in a more traditional manner, on the slopes of a rockery in the shared garden of No. 25.

But that is it, one lonely instance on a street as green as the Grove. This is a plant that was once ubiquitous. The emblem of a city, with beers named after it and songs sung to it. For most of the nineteenth century and the first half of the twentieth, London pride was *the* plant of the capital – twinned with the sparrow as an icon of East End fortitude, cheekily thriving in the grime and gloom. Noël Coward wrote *London Pride* after going to Paddington to catch a train and finding the station had been bombed in the night. He sat on a bench and watched while commuters stepped through the strewn glass. Amid the wreckage was a plucky wild flower and Coward remembered its common name: London pride. From there the song wrote itself, though setting it to the tune of 'Deutschland Uber Alles' was a masterstroke. Two days later it was sung in the West End for the first time.

There are similar stories. In December 1950 the American edition of *Vogue* gave five full pages to the gardening writer Beverley Nichols. His subject was sourcing plants for a flower bed dedicated to Joseph Nigg, a dead Austrian painter ('Try pitching that to Condé Nast today,' you might say. 'Try being as well connected as Beverley Nichols,' they might reply). Nichols collected London pride the day after the Luftwaffe blew up his house. Newly homeless, the author trudged to the ruins around St Pauls to write a story, but found himself unable to concentrate on the wreckage, so consumed was he with his own misfortune. Most regretted was the loss of a single hair that had grown on the head of Keats. Why, he wondered, had Hitler seen fit to sunder his connection with the poet? This self-pitying daze was thankfully broken by something growing, a verdant rosette on the edge of a smouldering pit. It was, of course, London pride, 'the Cockney weed, fresh as paint, impudently defying the might of the dictators...a specimen of which flew overhead at that very moment, spitting fire and threatening slaughter'.

Nichols took a sprig. He had never bothered before because it was everywhere. 'It grows,' he wrote, 'in the humblest gardens of the slums, spreading its flat glossy leaves in gloomy alleys, lifting its feathery pink blossoms through the fog.' But, he added that, if you were to tell a Cockney it had a Latin name, he would look at you suspiciously and tell you to 'come off it'. This was a plant of the humble, the downtrodden and the easily patronized.

In the 1830s Mary Howitt, most famous for *The Spider and the Fly* with its immortal opening line: 'Will you walk into my parlour? said a spider to a fly', wrote *The Poor Man's Garden*. It is predictable stuff: the rich man has grounds as far as the eye can see and they bring him no joy. The poor man rejoices in his simple flowers:

And pinks and clove-carnations,
Rich scented, side by side;
And at each end a hollyhock,
With an edge of London-pride.

Such Victorian sentimentality explains the disdain felt by our greatest-ever writer on rock gardens, Reginald Farrer

(1880–1920) for London pride. He admired the genus, noting that for 'value, ease, robustness of temper and stately charm… *Saxifraga* undoubtedly obliterates every other alpine race'. But he would not have sanctioned No.25 Grove Park's use of the plant as the centre of their rockery. He believed that 'the London Pride, or Pratting Parnell, or Prince's Feather, has its place only in the wildest, most worthless and outlying corners and rough margins of the rock-garden'.

I strongly disagree. I like my rockeries stuffed with London pride. At work, the assistant head gardener and I are in charge of weeding old rockeries and constructing new ones. We plant them as continuous mats of vegetation, punctured by outcrops of stone, like temples breaking through a jungle. Cheap, spreading plants are what we favour: great glaciers of snow-in-summer (*Cerastium tomentosum*), dismissed by Farrer as 'the universal grey-white chickweed used for edging'. We like waterfalls of creeping phlox (*Phlox subulata*), tumbling over the scree in waves of pink and lilac, and here Farrer would smile: he thought the day creeping phlox was introduced to Britain should be kept as a yearly festival. What Farrer would make of our other favourite plant, the hardworking stork's bill *Erodium* × *variabile*, a tiny trailing geranium, we will never know. It did not officially exist until 1980, seventy years after

253

he published his masterwork *The English Rock-Garden*, but knowing Farrer's views on commercially produced hybrids he would probably dismiss it as 'a mule', inferior in every way to its parents, *Erodium corsicum* and *Erodium reichardii*.

We 'staff' like to think of these rockeries as alpine, in the sense that they resemble a distant mountain range, with vegetation filling the valleys between the blown-bare ridges. Our employer, however, has a different and probably more authentic vision of alpine gardening. She would like to see her stone works as if they were chunks of *les Alpes de Haute Provence* cut free from the limestone cliffs and set down in Buckinghamshire. For her we plant pasque flowers (*Pulsatilla vulgaris*), the maiden pink (*Dianthus deltoides*), thrift (*Armeria maritima*) and the broadleaf stonecrop (*Sedum spathulifolium*). And, heartbreakingly, we occasionally cut back our racing mats of foliage into recognizable, separated, individual plants, pulling out London pride by the bucketful and making space for weeds to seed into.

My colleague, my client and I are the latest recruits to one hundred and twenty years of war. We professional gardeners are Robinsonians, setting out our alpines in the manner approved by the 19th century gardener and writer William Robinson, using massed drifts of colour to achieve a naturalistic effect.

Our employer is a Farrerite, in it for purity and the plants alone. In 1914, writing the foreword to another man's book, Farrer penned an attack on a Robinsonian garden, recognizable as belonging to the bonatist Sir Frank Crisp:

> What a display is here! You could do no better with coloured gravels. Neat unbroken blanks of first one colour and then another...it is not a rock garden...this is, in fact, nothing but the carpet bedding of our grandfathers...

Gosh. It stings. Me as well as Robinson. Sir Frank immediately swung a hatchet at Edward Augustus Bowles, the mild-mannered author who had asked Farrer to preface his latest work, publishing a pamphlet entitled: *Mr E A Bowles and his Garden: A New Parable of the Pharisee and the Publican*, which he distributed outside the Chelsea Flower Show.

At work our arguments are more peaceable. Every few months the gardeners are told that the rockeries need weeding, yet again, and that we should keep a better eye on them; and the gardeners reply, sotto voce, that we would never need weeding if we were allowed to cover them in London pride.

But at least we have it. I rarely see London pride in the gardens I pass. The days when it sprang from pavements and topped walls are long gone. From this we can infer that the plant was never a prolific self-seeder – it was no willow herb – and that it only escaped because it was planted in such prodigious quantities. Grove Park's lack of saxifrage is not the result of a changing climate but of changing tastes. No. 25 aside, there are no rock gardens on the street. Rockeries are no longer passé, they are period. Soon they will stop being a joke and become a curiosity. They are taking the path of the fernery, once a horticultural must-have, now a laminated signboard in a restored corner of some heritage garden.

Without full-time gardeners the imitation mountains I look after would slump back into their true form – sloping flower beds with stones on. The temperamental alpines would last only until it was discovered that blue 'Rozanne' geraniums and lime-yellow lady's mantle (*Alchemilla mollis*) make a good enough show without the need for constant weeding or dying at the first sign of rain in November. There would be a place for London pride – it alone could survive without our care – but the slope would be a rockery in the sense of being the place where the rocks were kept.

Reginald Farrer would barely be able to look at our attempts. They were not constructed on beds of free-draining clinker and dressed with sand, leafmould and limestone chips, as he insisted they ought to be. They were made from mud that happened to be hanging around and they are poorer for it. I get the feeling Farrer would also have hated me and hated this chapter's advice to plant cheap and en masse. The only thing I could do to further anger his ghost would be to start referring to saxifrages as 'rockfoils' and out myself as a true 'Ruskinian Faddist' suffering from a 'dismal and tedious affectation'.

These fine insults come from *The English Rock-Garden* and its series of asides about London's Wardour Street and the simple-minded intellectuals dwelling there, all of whom had been conned by the 'regrettable brummagem medievalism' of John Ruskin into calling campanulas bell-flowers. These flashes of personality make reading the book, which is essentially an encyclopaedia, an unexpected joy. In his introduction, Farrer promised 'to preserve the vivid and personal note, at any cost to the arid grey gravity usually considered necessary'. And warned that among the taxonomy and classification he would be including personal verdicts, which he hoped would anger fellow enthusiasts.

Farrer is now largely forgotten, but he lives on in books like the one you are reading. In her superlative biography of Reginald Farrer, *A Rage for Rock Gardening* (perhaps the best 'gardener's life' I have ever read), Nicola Shulman identifies

Farrer as the father of modern horticultural journalism: '[his] books changed garden writing for good...Farrer wrote as a personality, full of prejudice and indefensible opinions.' Gone was the omnipotent voice with its proclamations from on high, here was real human passion, along with its necessary attendants, disappointment and failure. By the age of twenty seven, Farrer had hit on a confident, chatty, erudite and informal style, so familiar to us that we forget how revolutionary it was. Take his description of the Bavarian gentian from *My Rock Garden*: '*Gentiana bavarica* is a beautiful little blue devil; so blue, and so beautiful; – and such a devil.' It's a sentence you could easily read in *Country Life* or *Hortus* today, but when considering the book in November 1907, *The Saturday Review* cited the passage for its informality, sniffing that the use of slang was 'cheap and fugitive' and that though 'Mr Farrer's garden-book might have been literature; we fear it must go among the tools.'

Many influential gardeners would disagree. Nicola Shulman finishes her short biography with examples of writers shaped by Farrer's prose, one of whom was Vita Sackville-West. I cannot help but think that Vita had the deeply troubled Reginald in mind when she wrote:

The whole point, I think, of the Alpines, as of certain people, is that in the rare moment of their blooming they transcend their tight habitual personality. They have something of the quality of the habitually silent reserved person who suddenly and without any warning exposes himself or herself in a single phrase of self-revelation, brief but beautiful. One knows it will not endure, but one has seen the light.

Farrer was a difficult and sensitive man, and practically mute until his mid-teens. Shulman writes that all his books, including the gardening ones, can be read as open letters of complaint to his parents. He died at forty, alone, drunk and collecting plants in the hills of Northern Burma, a half-written novel beside him. Farrer never became the great literary figure he longed to be, but his influence stretches over the twentieth century and beyond. To read his descriptions of *Anemone coronaria* or *Potentilla nitida* is to know that when he died and his little body was carried down the mountain, his voice remained, diffusing slowly out through the horticultural ether, working its way into the brains of Christopher Lloyd, Anna Pavord, Eleanor Perényi, Vita Sackville-West and countless others.

Reginald Farrer did not live to see London under attack from rockets – he died in 1920 – but he knew the destruction man was capable of and he would have understood why London pride took on a special significance. In 1918, with Europe in flames, he published *The Void of War,* a series of dispatches from the trenches. Farrer was not a soldier and came to the areas he covered after the fighting had passed, making the book a sort of travel guide to a maimed land. He arrives in what was once a village, sees bones sticking out of the mud, walks through long grass and weeds trying to avoid stepping in anything human, then moves on to the next shattered *localité*.

As Noël Coward and Beverley Nichols would later do, he finds himself clinging to the small beauties of nature, and in the ruins of the Château de Thièpval he finds a brave little purple-velvet petunia, all that was left of the once-great gardens and the world before the war. It prompts a thought: one day all this will be over. The shell holes and shrapnel will be cleared away and these years will become just an 'unmentionable episode in the life of a respectable château, once more clothed and in its right mind, with its ancestral haunts pressed back underground where they belong'. Farrer was desperately wrong. Thièpval could never be put back together – it had been blown to dust, the village obliterated, it lay on the Somme where a million men had died in five pointless months. There is nothing there now but memorials and fields where they still plough up skulls. Farrer had not noticed but the world had moved into a new era, one where streets, villages and towns could suddenly cease to be, one where no one would ever again castigate a garden writer for using slang. How utterly bizarre that just four years earlier he had lived in a continent at peace and gone to war over whether plants in a rockery should be allowed to touch each other.

The twentieth century rolled on without Farrer. From 1939 to 1945 the London County Council meticulously catalogued bomb damage to houses, businesses and public buildings. The results are in the Metropolitan Archives on a gorgeous series of Ordnance Survey maps. Each level of harm has been given its own colour. A structure filled in with solid black ink designates that it suffered total destruction. If coloured purple, it was damaged beyond repair, red and it was 'seriously damaged – doubtful if repairable'. Grove Park has twenty houses shaded a greenish-yellow, indicating 'blast damage – minor in nature'. Six are orange, the colour of more serious injury; these include the house behind the wisteria with which this book opened. Four are pink, 'seriously damaged – repairable at cost'. There is only one red house on the road and, despite its wounds, it still stands today.

Grove Park was lucky to escape. Just across the railway, another V2 did not blow up in the air but reached the ground and a whole neighbourhood disappeared. On the map there are twenty-one consecutive houses filled in with total-destruction black or beyond-repair purple. Today they are all gone. In their place is Warwick Gardens, a wedge of park with swings and a play slide, reached via a broad street that terminates after only a few buildings – all that remains of Azenby Road. The Grove feels so permanent, but it could so easily have gone. It is something I think about to bring a little perspective, when being chastised, again, for letting goose grass into the rockery.

# 18

# LAWN

In late summer, 'Nearly every woman who is lucky enough to own a lawn feels rising within her the determination to ask her friends to enjoy it.' So wrote Caroline French Benton, author of *A Little Cook Book for a Little Girl*, in 1907. In this simple sentence she strikes at the heart of the matter: a good lawn is nothing more than an invitation to enjoyment.

The quality of the grass does not matter. Oxford colleges have the world's best lawns. Each is a complement and comfort to the city's architecture; quadrangles of calm above which the spires can dream. Most are two-toned, with stripes of light and dark green. These lines are the wake of a lawnmower. Its heavy roller has pushed them sideways like a comb through wet hair. Looking with the grain, one sees bent blades and the light reflecting from them; against the grain, one faces the sliced tips and the shadows they create. Turn around and, as if by magic, the stripes will reverse their shades. These spaces give life to all that learning and must be as vital to the university as the Bodleian Library and the Clarendon Lab. But it is not the quality of the cut that invites us onto the lawn, it is the setting – the ancient walls of Headington stone, the swags of roses under leaded windows. Put the same square of grass on a roundabout and no one would care enough to visit it.

Which is one in the eye for pitch-care enthusiasts. No one really gives a fig about the density of the sward, what matters is the garden that surrounds it. No.4 Grove Park has the street's best lawn because there is enough grass to make sitting down look attractive and because it is sheltered by the leafy arms of two old magnolias. There are witch hazels and flowering currants (*Ribes sanguineum*) between the garden and the road, and rhododendrons and wisteria shade the house. The grassed area is a generous L-shape that is nibbled at from all sides by dusky cranesbill (*Geranium phaeum*) and Welsh poppies (*Papaver cambricum*). It is human-friendly, sheltered and inviting, and balm for the eyes after a day spent flickering in the city.

Lawns suffer terribly from being the default. They are unthinkingly applied to back gardens from fence to fence in a way that is both unsettling and uninviting. No one wants to lie on the ground between two stark verticals – you might as well be in the back of a lorry. Make the lawn smaller and plant good shrubs against the fences and a little tree that can swing its protective boughs over those lounging below. Smudge the boundaries further with mounds of herbaceous perennials and suddenly you have a lawn worth reclining on. It is no longer an operating table, it is a double bed scattered with cushions.

Garden designers wondering how large an area to turf or seed ought to invite clients to lie on the ground with their limbs spread. Every member of the household should be able to reach out and touch another without feeling cramped by them. Draw a line around the ensemble and you have the minimum area of grass required. Everything else can be bulbs and blossom trees. The lawn will not be too small; the real danger is in making it too exposed for comfort.

Last May, they cut Hyde Park weekly at six in the morning. A huge green tractor would drag a gang mower along, perfectly matching my speed as I cycled through on my way to work. It was a sensible policy; there were no people in the hours after dawn, just sleepy geese and feeding crows who dodge more quickly than picnickers. Riding back after my day's gardening, the park was always full of people sitting, drinking, eating and playing. But despite the open fields between Speakers' Corner and the Reformers' Tree, they all stuck close to the trees. Scale is important and we don't feel comfortable with things that dwarf us. This is what the eighteenth-century campaigners for 'Picturesque' gardens understood when they defied Capability Brown and his sweeping lawns and asked that the house be given some texture beyond bare grass, even if that meant thickets by the terrace steps. The feeling of being unsized by the landscape is instinctual; it is what Gustave Flaubert felt when he angrily noted, 'I feel completely bored…The Alps are out of all proportion to human existence. They are too big to be useful. This is the third time they have provoked a disagreeable reaction in me and I hope that it's the last.'

In that particular part of Hyde Park the grass is repeatedly obliterated by summer concerts and the Winter Wonderland fairground. After a few events, the ground becomes either compacted soil or mud, with hardly a living blade, and it is re-turfed. For fifteen months, a donor field in Lincolnshire will have been growing a green skin in readiness. It is scraped bare and driven down the A1 by the lorryload, finally being unrolled and grafted to the top of Central London.

What a wonderfully gratuitous use of materials. Universe-wide, grass is far more scarce than diamonds or uranium.

If aliens came to our planet and demanded we fill their ship with precious cargo, we would do better to stuff it with hay than with gold. Metal can be got from any solar system, a blade of grass is near miraculous. It is the result of a million chances, starting when a few particles in an interstellar space cloud met, formed a ball, dragged in gas and dust, and started the gravitational pile-on that made our sun, a star of just the right size. Other blessings for the lawn have included: Earth's perfect orbit; the appearance of water; the formation of the atmosphere; and the evolution of bacteria and archaea, prokaryotic life. To this we can add, after a further two billion years, the freakish event that led to one type of prokaryote living inside another, which set us on the way to moose, Mozart, grass, greenfinches and every complex form of eukaryotic organism that has ever lived.

Of course, the aliens would be just as happy with a hold full of thistles or pelargoniums, or even red valerian – all are equally unlikely – but we would not. Those plants can't be lounged on. Grass is magical because it survives the press of a human body. Its half-millimetre-thick blades keep living under the weight of an adult male and the book he's reading. They also take clipping in a way that most vegetation is physically unable to withstand. We could plant twenty thousand acorns skin to skin in an Oxford quad but as soon as our lawnmower meets the seedlings they will be dead, even on the highest setting. All plants grow from meristems, areas of undifferentiated cells that form leaves, stalks or flower components. Generally they are distributed throughout, with the highest concentration in the newer parts. When such a plant has its top chopped off, it must start again by branching somewhere lower down. Grasses grow differently, they have a base of intercalary meristems at ground level. A stem can be chopped in half and still continue to grow. It is being pushed up from beneath like toothpaste squeezed from a tube. Such growth is thought to be an evolutionary tactic to cope with grazing herbivores, but it also enables the plants to survive being cut with a lawnmower every Saturday morning.

Another solution for avoiding grazers is to grow slightly lower than your neighbours, the tactic employed by all our best lawn weeds. The highest biodiversity on Grove Park is in the lawn surrounding No.115. Here a three-storey building holds twenty-one flats built by the Metropolitan Police as staff accommodation. They have since been sold to The Soho Housing Association and are filled with all sorts of people, some of whom are children. This is the only front lawn on which people regularly play and they do so on a magical tapestry of grass, daisies, dandelions, vetch, yarrow, buttercups, celandine, clover and creeping cinquefoil. Each square foot seems to contain only a few inches of grass. In the wet weeks of late May, the whole mass of flower and leaf went up as quickly as bamboo, but each patch grew at its own rate, so that from above the whole lawn resembled the pillowy top of a green cloud.

The lawnmower will not help this diverse community. Its entire point is to weaken these broad-leaved plants with their distributed meristems and leave the grass to take over. But it seems that whoever looks after this lawn is in the admirable habit of cutting high, taking out the docks, brambles and thistles and letting the low-growing flowers get on with the business of life and pollination.

The enemies of the lawn are many. To them, lawns are seen as monocultural deserts that demand unsustainable levels of water, chemical feed and petrol. The criticism is justified. At work we keep fine lawns. For these we have an underground irrigation system, which shoots jets of water to rival any fountain Cardinal Ippolito ever commissioned for the Villa d'Este, but which comes on at two in the morning for only the owls and the foxes to enjoy. We have a cylinder lawnmower that cost five times my monthly salary; a verticutter to ensure our grass grows up, not sideways; a scarifier for removing dead blades and leaf sheaves; a hollow-tine machine that drives into the ground and removes tubes of soil, the holes to be filled with air or with the tons of kiln-dried sand we put down as a top dressing. In the summer months we go out and break the beads of dew with wide brushes to prevent moisture and fungus. We apply fertilizer from a hopper with a spinning propeller. There are absolutely no buttercups in these lawns.

But we also grow rough grass; places that are cut only once a year, sliced off in September with a reciprocating mower, or if my colleague has six days to spare, scythed down with a honed blade. These meadows are my joy. I love to walk in them and see what species are appearing and whether communities are fading or rising. We seeded heavily with yellow rattle (*Rhinanthus minor*) four years ago and the semi-parasitic annual has weakened the grass so that it no longer forms a damp mat by August. We have ox-eye daisies, knapweed, orchids, cow parsley, camassia, wild narcissus, stitchwort, vetches, bedstraws, cowslips, trefoils and scabious, with more plants finding their way in each year. It is glorious to look at but a pain to maintain – all that wild flower hay must be collected and stacked. The meadow is also not used for much more than walking in, which is wonderful if you have the acreage but not if it's your only outdoor space. The grass is too high and the flowers too rough to seduce people into lying on them. Picnics happen on shorter surfaces, and a game of football held there would be as practical as if it were underwater.

What is most useful, beautiful and environmentally friendly in a domestic garden is a lawn like that at No.115, a *laissez-faire* quilt of flowers, with some of the surprising plant communities of our meadow and most of the ball-rolling flatness of our croquet lawns. Thomas Maurice's 1799 ode to this land, *Grove-Hill: A Descriptive Poem* has a couplet that still holds the tiniest bit of truth today:

Rich meads, in Flora's gaudiest treasures bright,
And ever verdant lawns, the eye delight

In the high season at work we cut our fine turf at least twice a week. No.115 seems to be cut roughly every three weeks, the way it should be. In this part of London we are fortunate that there is no Saturday morning mowing cult. Grove Park may no longer resound to the rural symphonies (the naiad's call, the murmuring of a waterfall) that Maurice once heard, but at least our weekends are spared the continual up-and-down drone of 160cc engines. On this hill we prefer to listen to the police sirens down on Camberwell Church Street and the air ambulance roaring back to King's College Hospital.

The writer Eleanor Perényi had only two gardens in her life. The first, in Hungary, on the brow of the Carpathians, was 'the large and rather mournful park' attached to her husband's castle. Here the young Eleanor struggled in a savage climate to grow bulbs and introduce the perennials that she was never to see flower. As she planted she heard the guns of World War II booming above the mountains. Perhaps the daffodils bloomed after her family had fled; if so, they did so on a state farm. The Soviet Union had taken her flower beds.

The second garden was in America. She grieved the loss of her old land and vowed never to be attached to a piece of ground, but on the Connecticut coast the soil called and she reluctantly responded, slowly falling in love, until gardening became her greatest pleasure. After thirty years she told the story of her affair over seventy-two eclectic essays published as *Green Thoughts*. It was written, in part, to pass on everything she had learned, but also an act of preservation. In the foreword she writes:

As I look about me, I have reason to believe I belong to a vanishing species. Gardens like mine, which go by the unpleasing name of 'labor intensive,' are on their way out and before they go, I would like to contribute my penny's worth to their history.

Perényi is the only garden writer who makes me laugh out loud. She is best when looking with disdain at contemporary culture. Her piece on lawns is a strident defence of manicured sward. It should be cut with a push-along cylinder mower, with no gasoline fumes and engine roar, just the smell of clipped grass and the crescendo and diminuendo of whirring blades, so evocative of lost summer mornings and waking to hear, through the open window, someone else hard at work. She has no time for the natural lawn, which was fashionable even in 1981, writing that it looks 'as though one were too slatternly to keep a garden decent'.

However, she deeply regrets that this puts her on the side of the law. In many American communities it was illegal to let one's grass grow to disreputable lengths. Perényi was a horticultural Voltaire, disagreeing profoundly with the idea of turning her garden into a hayfield but ardently supporting those who went to court for the right. She also hated rotary lawnmowers and the kind of man who squatted over them, talking about carburettors and fuel lines and referring to his little Honda as 'she'. Here Perényi joins the line of counter-culturalists who have used the suburban dad cutting his lawn as a symbol of small-minded conformity. In turn this has spawned a counter-trope – the outwardly normal weekend mower, who waves to his neighbours and laughs at their jokes, but is in reality a drug-dealing kingpin, a mafia don or a secret agent in sleeper mode.

That secrets lie behind curtains just like yours is a seductive fantasy and Grove Park has more grounds than many to entertain these daydreams. On the 8th of February 1980 the investigative journalist Duncan Campbell published an article in *New Statesman* in which he claimed: 'A joint electronic surveillance and bugging facility for MI5, MI6 and the police is located in a quiet part of South London, at 113 Grove Park, Camberwell.' The facility, 'a large part of which is said by visitors to be below ground', was nondescript and 'entered by a driveway concealed behind a suburban terrace and overlooking a railway'. Campbell's account tallies with the large electric gate that still blocks that address, and the fact that this part of the road is not available to view on the stitched VR of Google Street View.

It is exciting to think that the little road I now consider mine is home to an underground nest of spies. I don't have any idea if it is true, but I won't dismiss it. Stranger things have happened – the evolution of grass, for one thing.

# 19

## ROSE

I started horticultural college knowing I would be a brilliant gardener. I had loose curly hair, wore shirts without collars and had read most of Thomas Hardy. I felt somehow sure these things bonded me with 'the land' in a way most people would never comprehend. My confidence fell away after a month, and I graduated fully aware of being an appalling gardener. How clichéd, to spend two years learning the most important lesson of all – that I still had a lot to learn.

Not that there aren't shortcuts. After a few terms I had a meeting with a television company. Two producers sat me down in a glass office and asked what I could bring to a new gardening programme. Probably not very much, I told them – I was still a student and didn't really know anything yet.

'That doesn't matter,' they laughed. 'Do you think Jamie knew everything about cooking? What's important is that you have a "thing". What's your thing?'

I must have looked blank. They elaborated: 'Are you the "rebel gardener"? Are you the "motorbiking gardener"? Are you the "northern gardener" or the "tattooed gardener"? What makes you different from the others we are going to see? What's your *thing*?'

Of course, I didn't have a thing. The 'collarless gardener' wouldn't do much, the 'Hardy-reading gardener' even less. I said I could be the cycling gardener but my heart wasn't in it and there was no enthusiasm from across the table. As I left they promised to get in touch with a date for the screen test, but they never did.

It wasn't the most embarrassing moment of my college days. That happened near Hanworth at the South West Middlesex Crematorium. Luckily, I hadn't confessed to any of the tutors that I had a profound bond with the soil that destined me for greatness, and they came to regard me as a student 'with his head screwed on'. As such, I was in charge of packing the van for placement days. That morning we were at the crematorium to learn about mulching roses. The lesson would be imparted as we spread manure under twelve hundred hybrid tea bushes in the Memorial Garden. Our drill was thus: one group to shovel manure into barrows, one group to wheel those barrows to the flower beds, and one group to spread it on the beds using a metal landscape rake. Except I did not pack the metal rakes – I packed the plastic leaf rakes. They bent if we pushed and did not hold when we pulled. All we could do was flick little half-handfuls of manure around while the tines caught on the roses and flung commemorative plaques about.

The cemetery staff laughed at the tutors for bringing such incompetents, and although my teachers were nice about it, I knew I had let them down. Which, I think, is why even today I feel a pang of disappointment whenever I see a hybrid tea rose. But I am not alone in this. No one fashionable likes hybrid teas anymore.

The hybrid tea is the familiar rose of the valentine bouquet. Its petals rise into a point at the centre of the bloom, with those to the outside curling slightly as they unfurl. The buds are held singly and upright on thick stems above sparse foliage. This is a traditional front-garden plant and was once by far and away the most popular rose in Britain and America. It is still grown well at several houses on the Grove, that is right at the front and pruned back annually to fence-level, ensuring its new growth and flowers are on display for all and that the ugly framework is only seen by the homeowner. The hybrid tea's fall from pre-eminence began with a trend towards roses with a softer silhouette. These 'old-fashioned' plants were romantic – they could flounce, drape and swoon. No hybrid tea was ever caught billowing, and a further wound for the awkward plants came in the widespread belief that they had no fragrance. It's not true, some do, but in many hybrid teas this trait was lost as breeders chased ever-brighter shades of white, yellow, red and orange.

It is a pity that the hybrid tea is unreliably scented. Some of its ancestors are the most fragrant flowers in cultivation. Roses are fantastic breeders, with species able to cross readily and produce fertile offspring. Carl Linnaeus, father of botany and the taxonomic system used by gardeners and scientists alike, noted this in his *Species Plantarum* of 1753: 'The species of the genus *Rosa* are difficult to distinguish and determine, I have the impression that nature combines just for fun a number of them and then forms a new one out of the lot.'

Our modern roses mostly contain genetic material from just ten wild species. Some will be close to their parents; a modern floribunda rose like 'The Fairy' is a cross between a rambling multiflora rose from Eastern Asia (*Rosa multiflora*) and the China rose (*Rosa chinensis*). Others have muddier ancestry. Hybrid teas combine strands of China rose DNA with others from the Gallic rose (*Rosa gallica*), the musk rose (*Rosa moschata*), *Rosa gigantea* from the Himalayan foothills and the Kyrgyzstani repeat-flowerer, *Rosa fedtschenkoana*. That all of these exotic strangers now grow on Grove Park is exciting, that they do so in a single small bush at No.83 is almost a miracle. But roses are by far the most common woody plant on the street, and on The Grove we will also have elements of the European dog rose (*Rosa canina*), the Persian yellow rose (*Rosa foetida*), *Rosa phoenicia* from the Caucusus Mountains, *Rosa rugosa* from the coastal sand dunes of Siberia and Korea, and its inland neighbour, the carpeting *Rosa lucieae*.

The diversity of DNA in modern roses ensures that there is a colour and habit for almost every situation. The hybrid tea 'Tequila Sunrise' has petals that glow gold at their base and grenadine-red at their tips, creating a wonderfully lurid display that would never be allowed at Sissinghurst, where the first living thing set in the ground by Vita Sackville-West and Harold Nicolson was the noisette rose 'Madame Alfred Carrière', a vigorous white climber with perfect green leaves and a pink blush to the fresh-opened petals. I hope that Vita was not such a snob that she would sneer at 'Tequila Sunrise' in the garden of someone who truly loved it. After all, when writing of another novelty, the green-flowered *Rosa chinensis*

'Viridiflora', she captured the essential truth of all rose-growing: 'Either you love it or you have no use for it; it all depends on what you feel.'

Vita Sackville-West wrote enchantingly of her experiences as a land girl during the Great War, picking through gardens that had been left to seed by owners called away or killed. In these newly wild places the roses, even the hybrid teas, were not scrimping, scrubby things but wildly blossoming shrubs. Their master had gone and with him the voice of the experts who whispered always, 'Prune…cut almost to the ground… be pitiless, be ruthless…snub them as hard as you can, even as Victorian parents snubbed their children.' Without being bullied, maimed or stunted by the gardener's knife, each plant was free to grow lavishly and toss its head about as Vita believed it was meant to.

'Don't interfere with the roses' should be printed on the handle of every pair of secateurs, just as 'Smoking causes cancer' is on a packet of tobacco. We are detrimentally obsessed with rose pruning. In our second year of college, my classmates and I returned to the South West Middlesex Crematorium to prune the memorial roses. We lined up each cut as carefully as if the stems had been wires on a bomb, placing and removing the blades, testing the resistance of the spring, before finally closing our eyes and making the snip. We were cutting for health, taking out any diseased wood and pruning to an outward-facing bud. We made every slice at forty-five degrees so the ends would shed water. It was all very serious and extremely professional and at no point did I ask myself if these plants would be best cut down to six-inch sticks every winter. I'm sure Vita Sackville-West has not gone to hell, but if she has, then a part of her punishment will be to spend every February in a cemetery in Metroland, watching student horticulturalists climb off the minibus from Acton and unthinkingly butcher a thousand roses.

The need to *do* causes more damage in gardens than benign neglect ever has. Romance is a thin paint and is built up in layers. No serendipitous mingling of branch and bloom can happen if the gardener acts as an overbearing chaperone, slapping away shrubs as soon as they look at each other. There can be no beauty in the cracks if everything is weeded the second it appears. It is awful to judge the value of a garden by how much work it is to maintain. Vita's lavishness is pruned away every time someone waves a chainsaw just for the sake of it, and the glorious, species-specific idiosyncrasies of the plants are often never seen because the gardener has filled his shed, his head and his afternoons with hedge trimmers.

Our England is a garden, and such gardens are not made
By singing:--"Oh, how beautiful!" and sitting in the shade,
While better men than we go out and start their working lives
At grubbing weeds from gravel-paths with broken dinner-
   knives.

So wrote Rudyard Kipling in his poem *The Glory of the Garden*. He is wrong. Lounging under the trees is an essential horticultural job. It is while the gardener lies reading that his garden matures, and if anything has gone so drastically wrong in the flower beds that he is distracted from his book, then he knows it is time to act. Discard Kipling's garden and take up Andrew Marvell's. In his poem *The Garden*, he despairs of man and his incessant labour, always struggling to win a spare and spiky crown of laurel, when if he just turned from the struggle and lay in the grass, he would find Nature ready to weave far better garlands over his cushioned head, 'Annihilating all that's made / To a green thought in a green shade.'

Of course this style of gardening is easier when one has the space for it. If old-fashioned roses were left unmolested, they would entirely swallow a front garden the size of most on Grove Park. But where there is space for some exuberance is on the bricks of the front wall. At No.83 there is a large-flowered floribunda that is always the street's first rose to open in May. Roses do not completely cover a wall, no matter how artfully they have been wired and no matter what Vita Sackville-West, who wanted every post-war prefab house in England to be hidden behind a curtain of her beloved *Rosa* 'Madame Alfred Carrière', might have thought. This means roses must work with their support. Anything will complement the honey-toned limestone of the Cotswolds, but red bricks can clash with yellow or scarlet petals. Those bright colours suit pale Bath or Portland stone better, or even a simple coat of white masonry paint. Bright pink roses look good on wooden cladding or fences, and pale pink climbers complement everything man has ever built.

We have to wait until July for the Grove's best and biggest rose to come into flower. It is a vast white climber growing at No.98. The house is one half of a pretty little pair, the exact mirror image of its conjoined neighbour. Both houses have solid, square-columned bay windows and deep-set porches under a shared first-storey half-roof. It's on these old tiles that the rose basks in the light from the south. It rises between the front doors on a stem so ancient and thick that it has become a trunk, before splitting in two directions underneath a decorative stone finial. Half of its flowers are portioned to the house on the right, half to the left. In all it stretches twenty-five feet, thrusting blooms up in front of four French casements. Technically it is owned by No.98, and looking at the rest of that garden, a mass of attractive single-flowered roses behind a dipping hedge of evergreen Darwin's barberry (*Berberis darwinii*), it is clear that it has been chosen according to that household's taste, but its function is communal. It is an equal ornament to both houses. The Victorian builder who set out to create a vision of symmetry will be smiling down on this neighbourly act of lending, unless, of course, he was a hybrid tea man who preferred his roses six inches from the ground where they couldn't tap at any window panes.

In *The English Flower Garden* of 1893, William Robinson lamented that roses were seen only as a decorative vase flower, and that every nurseryman's catalogue described them by their blooms alone. Why, he wondered, could they not be understood as growing plants? He admonished his contemporaries for timidly lining up their roses in the cutting garden, as if they were a crop to be hidden away and brought to the table when needed. To those who worried that roses would look scrappy when not in flower or leaf, he replied that the enforced primness of plants was 'as unnatural as children who never have grubby fingers or wrinkled collars'.

But the hybrid tea rose belongs to a part of the world where children *do* stand up straight with their cheeks washed and their hair combed, even if only on Sundays and for half an hour before tea. It is a plant of the front parlour, a flower in its best skirt that has been allowed in to sit with the adults. In 1940, the Coca-Cola Company ran an American advertising campaign centred around the phrase 'Flowers make a house a home.' Hybrid tea roses featured heavily in the advertising, with perfect vases of red blooms sitting alongside advertising copy that brightly announced:

> Everybody welcomes those things that brighten a home, that make it a pleasant place to be and see. Flowers, pleasantly arranged, add to the spirit of living. So does ice-cold Coca-Cola.

For ten cents readers could send off for a book by Laura Lee Burroughs in her series *Flower Arranging: A Fascinating Hobby*. The introduction to volume two begins:

> We all like to have our homes admired…when friends visit our house or apartment it is pleasant to have them enthusiastic about the excellent food, the original table

decorations and the attractive flower arrangements…one woman may be famous for her smoked turkey, another for her superlative hash: one may make a beautiful table with green orchids…

And so it continues. After fifty pages of inspirational displays the book concludes with an important message: 'Now that flower arranging has become almost a cult, and women are demonstrating their talents with flowers, entertaining has taken on added significance…for every form of entertaining, Coca-Cola is, of course, essential.' There follows twelve full-colour pictures showing how to arrange the drinks as if they were dahlias. Alongside a vase of pink flowers, a silver soup tureen stands filled with vials of dark liquid. The caption reads, 'The gardening club is coming – quantities of ice-cold bottles of Coca-Cola are ready, and so are the Rubrum Lilies.' Next, a trio of bottles stands by a blowsy pelargonium and a bowl of nibbles: 'A game of bridge is in progress – and of course, Coca-Cola is nearby on the best flower table.' Coca-Cola is also shown sitting in a flower pot while it waits for a game of badminton to finish, next to some zinnias, with some marigolds ('Autumn in the country!'), and, of course, filling a wheelbarrow in a rose garden.

This is the world the hybrid tea inhabits, more real to the plant than its growing days out in the garden. It sits in the kind of interior Harold Nicolson complained about when he wrote home to Vita about the taste of the wealthy Americans he was meeting:

> I do not see any of these millionaire libraries being diversified by a bit of stone from Persepolis, some bass left about, Martin's latest bone, Tikki, a hammer, a Rodin, a tobacco tin full of seeds, some loose films, a back number of the *New Statesman*, an evening shoe on its way back to the bedroom, and a soda water syphon. Yet it is these varied and illuminating objects that make our rooms real and personal.

This passage perfectly captures the Sissinghurst aesthetic, inside and out. The old rose is to a garden what a dented cigar case full of Roman nails is to a bookshelf. It gives the impression of comfortable antiquity, of a bond with place that goes back generations, even if that isn't remotely true. In its own way it is just as confected as the overbred hybrid tea or sideboard set out with ice-cold cola, but it looks dreamy while it's about it. Laura Lee Burroughs and her book *Flower Arranging* are an interesting, if rather fusty, footnote in the history of rapidly changing America. She had a son, William S, who also wrote, sometimes about coke 'with a small 'c'', and went on to be one of the most controversial authors of the twentieth century.

Harold Nicolson further elaborates on the essential nature of Sissinghurst in another letter to his wife, this one dated the 26th of October 1948:

Sissinghurst has a quality of mellowness, of refinement, of unflaunting dignity, which is just what we wanted to achieve and which in some ways we have achieved by chance. I think it is mainly due to the succession of privacies: the forecourt, the first arch, the main court, the tower arch, the lawn, the orchard. All a series of escapes from the world, giving the impression of cumulative escape.

Everyone should have the right to escape from the world, even if they don't possess a tower, a court, or even an orchard. The houses on the Grove are lucky to have front gardens, and the best of them are those that provide a series of veils between private life and busy existence. The houses that have replaced their gardens with parking spaces have an unbroken connection with the road beyond. From there they are linked to all of London, good and bad – the hospitals, the nightclubs, the traffic jams and the bus lanes. If they had kept a garden, they would have barriers. No.98 has its berberis hedge, its green-fringed path and its protective wall rose, a screen that is physically thin but psychologically priceless.

In our back garden we grow five roses, all of them too big for the space. In an old apple tree we have Lady Banks' yellow rose (*Rosa banksiae* 'Lutea'). The shed is covered in a deep pink rose, newly bred in the old-fashioned style, *Rosa* 'Harlow Carr'. One ivy-covered fence explodes with the climbing form of the bourbon rose 'Souvenir de la Malmaison', its stems arching out to drop petals over the centre of the lawn. Opposite is a vigorous rambler 'American Pillar' that flowers once a year in bright cerise. It bloomed in Kat's parents' garden on the day we were married and we took a cutting, meaning that each June we have eight hundred simple pink flowers to remind us to go and buy an anniversary card. Finally, there is 'Malvern Hills', a repeat-flowering yellow rambler whose blossom fades to white as it ages, bringing light to the shadowed back fence.

All are tied in but never cut down. In midsummer we lie on the grass with books and drinks, with all the unpruned roses throwing their petals about. In those moments I allow myself to think briefly, as I did all those years ago, that I am a *brilliant* gardener.

## 20

## DREAMS

Back when people still remembered his name, decades before his Camberwell garden sprouted houses and the pavements I now walk, there was an anecdote told about Dr John Coakley Lettsom. If the soil froze and the farm men went hungry, he would employ them at Grove Hill. In the dead of winter there was little for them to do but slouch between the Observatory and the mermaid statues. One morning the doctor was chided by a neighbour for keeping so many men in idleness. 'True, neighbour,' said the doctor, with a smile of complacency. 'But who pays them? You or I?'

Dr Lettsom understood the physical damage and mental strain caused by poverty. Another tale celebrates his visit to an ailing woman who was struggling and beaten by life. Once done, he scribbled a note on his prescription pad and delivered it to the parish clerk. It read, 'A shilling per diem for Mrs Moreton. Money, not physic, will cure her.'

Grove Park is an affluent street in an area of high inequality. To the south of the Grove, Lettsom's name has been taken by the Lettsom Gardens Association, which lovingly manages a community space and woodland, and the Lettsom Allotments Association, with thirty-five plots and a small orchard. To the north the doctor gave his name to the Lettsom Gz, a subsection of the Pecknarm Young Gunners, themselves a splinter of the murderous Peckham Boys gang. 'Pecknarm' is a phonetic portmanteau of Peckham and Vietnam – these streets are a warzone. The Lettsom Gardens and the Lettsom Gz are a reminder that we all walk the same streets in different cities. While I look at forsythia, others are on patrol.

There are hidden stories in everything. This book has tried to share a few that relate to Grove Park, but many are left untold. There is the history of the squat at No.2, which in the early nineties named itself Groove Park and where according to one visitor, 'Human-sized ducks hang from the ceiling… industrial waste grows into metal sculptures and the walls have been decorated by a dozen Jackson Pollocks.' We could go back to 1969 when No.100 was an art commune with a young

Brian Eno sleeping on a bookshelf. Or to the Camber Well itself, source of the waters that give this area its name, which reputedly lies behind one of the houses. But these are legends of Grove Park bedrooms and back gardens, and will have to find their own historian. Mine has been an odyssey on the public pavement and I have enjoyed each step of it.

This is not to suggest that every garden on Grove Park is a joy. There are plenty with big cars and nothing else, profoundly sad places, all of them. This account has chosen to ignore them. To quote one last letter from Harold to Vita:

Life is such a difficult and cruel thing, so why make it more difficult by gossiping about people's faults? There is beauty, and love, in this world, and intelligence and virtue – why lunch at the Ritz and spend your time picking out the ugly things?

When Sol was six months old he was able to recognize our front door, and would shout excitedly at it when we turned onto the path. Soon after he learned to recognize the lax leaves of our lime tree hedge, even when they turned butter yellow, and he would start chattering from halfway down the street. What a compliment – he wanted to be inside with us. Of course, once in he would bang on the door to be let out and wail forlornly. He is just a baby who likes change. In which case he would do well to continue plodding around Grove Park with his dad. Front gardens are ever in flux. They combine the innate seasonality of plants with the capriciousness of human life. Some will change with fashion, others have found their look and will stick with it, the plants and the people who care for them growing older together. The cherries will bloom again. People will move out and others move in. Sol and I could walk the street every morning and night until I'm ninety and find new things each time. Sadly for me he'll have better things to do with his teens, twenties, thirties and forties, but perhaps we could take a stroll each spring to check on the magnolias.

While writing this book I was asked which of the gardens on the Grove was my favourite. There are a few I particularly care for, and I hope that comes across in my writing, but none is a clear front-runner. Instead I answer the question with what I would do if I ever had a Grove Park garden of my own. This imaginary space is the ½ garden of this book's title, one that is almost real because it goes everywhere with me.

I would take one of the houses with a paved front garden and smash through to the clay of Camberwell, keeping an eye out for water mains and anthracite coal. Next, I would set the hard landscaping: a path, a gate and a low wall with fleur-de-lis railings. The gate would be in the corner diagonally opposite the front door and the path would run between them in an S. I want to stretch the time spent between street and home. On the side of the path away from the house there would be a tiny patch of grass and spring bulbs, with a small wooden bench facing the gate, a reminder that this is a human space. On the other side of the path I'd have the cursed wheelie bins under a pergola with a winemaker's grapevine, perhaps 'Bacchus', growing over it. The rest would all be flower bed with hardy geraniums, domes of old-fashioned roses, *Alchemilla mollis*, and anything else that looked like blowing in and surviving. Along the railings at the front I'd grow *Wisteria sinensis*, and behind that I'd have some leggy shrubs, perhaps laburnum and a dark-flowered lilac. Finally, on the house I'd train a soft pink climbing rose like 'New Dawn'. Nothing would be evergreen because I am addicted to bud burst and the in-out breath of the seasons. My house would be a mournful sight at dusk in December. But it's only two months between the reddening of the vine and the breaking of the snowdrops, and we could spend that time on the sofa with our curtains firmly closed.

# AUTHOR'S
# ACKNOWLEDGEMENTS

My greatest thanks to Skevoulla Gordon – this would be half a book without her illustrations. Thanks also to the residents of Grove Park. I hope you don't mind me sharing your street with the world? If you noticed the loitering stranger with the red pram, take this as reassurance that I was not a burglar – I was only stealing ideas.

At Octopus I would like to thank Alison Starling for her encouragement and for making this project happen. Also, Sybella Stephens for her work on the text, and Jonathan Christie for his work on the design.

I owe an unpayable debt to my parents. To Ronald Dark for giving me a love of history and a sense of humour. To Ruth Sander for always encouraging me to write. I must also thank Allan and Barbara Johnson for their unfailing support. None of this would have been possible without my wife Kat who tolerated my getting up at 4am to think about buddleja and suffered through my tedious exhaustion while working, being the perfect mother and bringing light and cheer to South East London.

# BIBLIOGRAPHY

## BOOKS

Naoko Abe, *'Cherry' Ingram: The Englishman Who Saved Japan's Blossoms* (Vintage, 2019)

Anonymous, *Jenny's Geranium; or, the Prize Flower of a London Court* (SW Partridge, 1869)

William Black, *Madcap Violet* (Macmillan & Co, 1876)

William Blake, *Songs of Innocence and Experience* (William Blake, 1794)

James Boswell, *The Life of Samuel Johnson* (C Dilly, 1791)

E A Bowles, *My Garden in Spring* (T C & E C Jack, 1914)

Richard Bradley, *An Archaeology of Natural Places* (Routledge, 2000)

Christopher Brickell and David Joyce, *The Royal Horticultural Society: Pruning & Training* (Dorling Kindersley, 1996)

Henry Bright, *The English Flower Garden* (Macmillan and Co, 1881)

James Britten and Robert Holland, *A Dictionary of English Plant-Names* (Trübner & Co, 1886)

John Burroughs, *Winter Sunshine* (Hurd and Houghton, 1876)

Laura Lee Burroughs, *Flower Arranging: A Fascinating Hobby* (The Coca-Cola Co, 1940)

Maggie Campbell-Culver, *The Origin of Plants: The People and Plants that Have Shaped Britain's Garden History* (Headline, 2001)

Samuel Taylor Coleridge, *The Complete Poems* (Penguin Classics, 1997)

Nicholas Culpeper, *A Physical Directory, or a Translation of the London Dispensatory* (Peter Cole, 1649)

Barry Day (Ed.), *The Letters of Noël Coward* (Bloomsbury, 2008)

Elizabeth Story Donno (Ed.), *Andrew Marvell: The Complete Poems* (Penguin Classics, 1972)

Alexandre Dumas, *La Dame aux Camélias* (Calmann-Lévy, 1848)

Paul Farley (Ed.), *John Clare: Poems* (Faber & Faber, 2016)

Reginald Farrer, *The Void of War: Letters from Three Fronts* (Constable & Co, 1918)

Reginald Farrer, *The English Rock-Garden* (T C & E C Jack, 1919)

C R L Fletcher and Rudyard Kipling, *A School History of England* (Henry Frowde and Hodder & Stoughton, 1911)

Richard Folkard, *Plant Lore, Legends, and Lyrics* (Sampson Low, Marston, Searle, and Rivington, 1884)

Robert Fortune, *Three Years' Wandering in the Northern Provinces of China..., A Visit to the Tea, Silk, and Cotton Countries, with an Account of the Agriculture and Horticulture of the Chinese, New Plants, etc.* (John Murray, 1847)

Robert Fortune, *A Journey to the Tea Countries of China; Including Sung-Lo and the Bohea Hills, with a Short Notice of the East India Company's Tea Plantations in the Himalaya Mountains* (John Murray, 1852)

Robert Fortune, *Yedo and Peking; A Narrative of a Journey to the Capitals of Japan and China, with Notices of the Natural Productions, Agriculture, Horticulture and Trade of Those Countries and Other*

*Things Met with by the Way* (John Murray, 1863)

Peter Furtado (Ed.), *Great Cities Through Travellers' Eyes* (Thames & Hudson, 2019)

Dan Pearson, *Home Ground: Sanctuary in the City* (Conran Octopus, 2011)

John Gerard, *The Herball: Or Generall Historie of Plantes* (J Norton, 1597)

Bob Gilbert, *Ghost Trees: Nature and People in a London Parish* (Saraband, 2018)

Louise Glück, *The Wild Iris* (Ecco, 1992)

Charlotte Perkins Gilman, *The Yellow Wall-Paper, Herland, and Selected Writings* (Penguin Classics, 1999)

Sir Harry Godwin, *The History of the British Flora* (Cambridge University Press, 1956)

D G Hessayon, *The Flowering Shrub Expert* (Expert Books, 1994)

Robert Hogg, *British Pomology* (Groombridge and Sons, 1851)

Maureen Howard (Ed.), *Edith Wharton: Collected Stories 1891–1910* (Library of America, 2001)

Derek Jarman, *Modern Nature* (Century, 1991)

Edward Kemp, *How to Lay Out a Garden* (Bradbury and Evans, 1858)

John Coakley Lettsom, *History of Some of the Effects of Hard Drinking: The Sixth Edition* (C Dilly, 1791)

John Coakley Lettsom, *Hints for Promoting a Bee Society* (Darton and Harvey, 1796)

John Coakley Lettsom, *The Naturalist's and Traveller's Companion* (C Dilly, 1799)

John Coakley Lettsom, *Grove-Hill: A Rural and Horticultural Sketch* (S Couchman, 1804)

Amy Levy, *A London Plane-tree and Other Verse* (T Fisher Unwin, 1889)

Richard Mabey, *Food for Free* (Collins, 1972)

Charles Mackay, *Extraordinary Popular Delusions and the Madness of Crowds* (Richard Bentley, 1841)

Thomas Maurice, *Grove-Hill:
A Descriptive Poem, With an
Ode to Mithra* (1799)

Peter McHoy, *A Practical Guide
to Pruning* (Eagle Editions,
2001)

Leonard Meager, *The English
Gardener, or, A Sure Guide to
Young Planters and Gardeners*
(P Parker, 1670)

Vladimir Nabokov, *Speak, Memory:
An Autobiography Revisited*
(Weidenfeld & Nicolson, 1967)

L Hugh Newman, *Butterfly Farmer*
(Phoenix House, 1953)

John Nichols, *Illustrations of the
Literary History of the Eighteenth
Century* (Nichols, Son & Bentley,
1817)

Nigel Nicolson (ed.), *Vita and
Harold: The Letters of Vita
Sackville-West and Harold
Nicolson 1910–1962* (Weidenfeld
& Nicolson, 2018)

Anna Pavord, *The Tulip*
(Bloomsbury, 1999)

Eleanor Perényi, *Green Thoughts:
A Writer in the Garden*
(Pimlico, 1994)

Henry Phillips, *Flora Historica:
Or, the Three Seasons of the British
Parterre* (E Lloyd & Son, 1829)

Charles E Raven, *English Naturalists
from Neckam to Ray: A Study of
the Making of the Modern World*
(Cambridge University Press,
2010)

William Robinson, *The English
Flower Garden and Home Grounds*
(John Murray, 1893)

J K Rowling, *Harry Potter and the
Philosopher's Stone*
(Bloomsbury, 1997)

Vita Sackville-West, *The Land*
(William Heinemann, 1926)

Sir Edward Salisbury, *Weeds &
Aliens* (The New Naturalist,
1961)

Sir George Sitwell, *An Essay on
the Making of Gardens: Being
a Study of Old Italian Gardens,
of the Nature of Beauty, and the
Principles Involved in Garden
Design* (John Murray, 1909)

Nicola Shulman, *A Rage for Rock
Gardening: The Story of Reginald
Farrer, Gardener, Writer and Plant
Collector* (Short Books, 2002)

Alfred, Lord Tennyson, *Poems, Chiefly Lyrical* (Effingham Wilson, 1830)

Alfred, Lord Tennyson, *In Memoriam* (Edward Moxon, 1850)

Edward Thomas, *Collected Poems* (Faber & Faber, 1921)

Robert Tyas, *The Sentiment of Flowers; Or Language of Flora* (Houlston & Stoneman, 1842)

Gilbert White, *The Natural History and Antiquities of Selborne* (T Bensley for B White and Son, 1789)

Roma White, *'Twixt Town and Country: A Book of Suburban Gardening* (Harper & Bros., 1900)

Anne Wilkinson, *The Passion for Pelargoniums: How They Found Their Place in the Garden* (The History Press, 2007)

Walter P Wright, *The Perfect Garden* (Grant Richards, 1908)

## PAPERS

Anne Bruneau, Julian R Starr and Simon Joly, 'Phylogenetic relationships in the genus *Rosa*: New evidence from chloroplast DNA sequences and an appraisal of current knowledge' in *Systematic Botany*, Vol. 32, 2 (2007)

Zhe Chen, Yang Niu, Chang-Qiu Liu and Hang Sun, 'Red flowers differ in shades between pollination systems and across continents' in *Annals of Botany*, Vol. 126, 5 (2020)

Marie Fougère-Danezan, Simon Joly, Anne Bruneau, Xin-Fen Gao and Li-Bing Zhang, 'Phylogeny and biogeography of wild roses with specific attention to polyploids' in *Annals of Botany*, Vol. 115, 2 (2015)

Thomas B Gilmore, 'James Boswell's Drinking' in *Eighteenth-Century Studies*, Vol. 24, 3 (1991)

Christelle Guédot, Peter J Landolt and Constance L Smithhisler, 'Odorants of the flowers of butterfly bush, *Buddleja davidii*, as possible attractants of pest species of moths' in *Florida Entomologist*, vol. 91, 4 (2008)

Bernd Heinrich, 'Rapid flower-opening in *Iris pseudacorus*' in *Northeastern Naturalist*, Vol. 22, 3 (2015)

Penelope Hunting, 'Dr John Coakley Lettsom, Plant-Collector of Camberwell' in *Garden History*, Vol. 34, 2 (Winter, 2006)

Qun Li, JinLong Bao, XueYing Wang, XuHui Chen, ChengJiang Ruan, 'Nectar compositions and insect pollination of *Althaea rosea*' in *Journal of Shenyang Agricultural University*, Vol. 42, 2 (2011)

L A Lodwick, 'Evergreen plants in Roman Britain and beyond: movement, meaning and materiality' in *Britannia*, 48 (2017)

Nicolas J Vereecken, Achik Dorchin, Amots Dafni, Susann Hötling, Stefan Schulz and Stella Watts, 'A pollinators' eye view of a shelter mimicry system' in *Annals of Botany*, Vol. 111, 6 (2013)

Steven Vogel, 'Twist-to-bend ratios of woody structures' in *Journal of Experimental Botany*, Vol. 46, 289 (1995)

Ruohan Wang, Sai Xu, Xiangyu Liu, Yiyuan Zhang, Jianzhong Wang and Zhixiang Zhang, 'Thermogenesis, flowering and the association with variation in floral odour attractants in *Magnolia sprengeri* (Magnoliaceae)' in *PLOS ONE*, Vol. 9, 6 (2014)

Ruohan Wang and Zhixiang Zhang, 'Floral thermogenesis: An adaptive strategy of pollination biology in Magnoliaceae' in *Communicative & Integrative Biology*, Vol. 8, 1 (2015)

John Warren and Sally Mackenzie, 'Why are all colour combinations not equally represented as flower-colour polymorphisms?' in *New Phytologist*, Vol. 151, 1 (2001)

V Wissemann and C M Ritz, 'Evolutionary patterns and processes in the genus *Rosa* (Rosaceae) and their implications for host-parasite co-evolution' in *Plant Systematics and Evolution*, Vol. 266, 1/2, Evolution of Rosaceae (2007)

Jan Woudstra, 'The Italian Garden at Chiswick House' in *English Heritage Historical Review*, Vol. 5 (2010)

Alexandros Xafis, Juha Saarinen, Katharina Bastl, Doris Nagel and Friðgeir Grímsson, 'Palaeodietary traits of large mammals from the middle Miocene of Gračanica (Bugojno Basin, Bosnia-Herzegovina)' *Palaeobiodiversity and Palaeoenvironments*, Vol. 100 (2020)

# INDEX